Mute Vol 2 #6

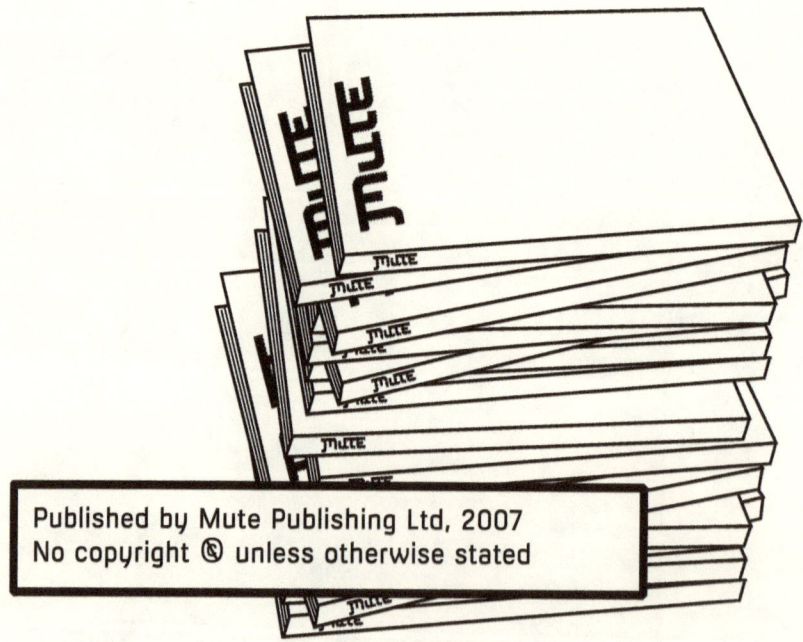

EDITOR
Josephine Berry Slater <josie@metamute.org>

DEPUTY EDITOR
Benedict Seymour <ben@metamute.org>

ASSISTANT EDITOR
Anthony Iles <anthony@metamute.org>

EDITORIAL BOARD
Josephine Berry Slater, Matthew Hyland
<infuriant@autistici.org>, Anthony Iles, Demetra
Kotouza <demetra@inventati.org>, Hari Kunzru
<hari@metamute.org>, Pauline van Mourik
Broekman, Benedict Seymour, Laura Sullivan
<alchemical44@yahoo.co.uk> and
Simon Worthington

PUBLISHERS
Pauline van Mourik Broekman
<pauline@metamute.org>
Simon Worthington <simon@metamute.org>

ISSUE DESIGN
Simon Worthington, Laura Oldenbourg
<laura_oldenbourg@yahoo.com> and OSP
http://ospublishing.constantvzw.org
Designed using 100% FLOSS tools, thanks to:
ScriBus, Gimp, Inkscape, FontForge and
OpenOffice.

ADVERTISING & MARKETING
Sarah Bailey <sarah@metamute.org>

WEBSITE
Metamute.org is powered by Drupal and
CiviCRM FLOSS Software, with additional
software services by our very own OpenMute
http://openmute.org

TECH SUPPORT
Website upgrade: Greenman at Code+
Web infrastructure: Darron Broad
<darron@kewl.org>

INTERNS
Special thanks to: Esiri Erheriene-Essi and Eva van
Ingen for legal support on our Networked
Distribution system, http://agents.metamute.org

ADMINISTRATOR
Sam Gul <sam@metamute.org>

COVER
Concept: Anthony, Ben and Josie; realisation:
Richard at Happy Retouching and
Simon Worthington

OFFICE
Mute, Unit 9, The Whitechapel Centre,
85 Myrdle Street, London E1 1HQ, UK
T: +44 (0)20 7377 6949
F: +44 (0)20 7377 9520
email: <mute@metamute.org>

SUBSCRIPTIONS
Sam Gul
T: +44 (0)20 7377 6949
F: +44 (0)20 7377 9520
email: <subs@metamute.org>
web: http://www.metamute.org/subs/

DISTRIBUTION UK
Central Books, 99 Wallis Road, London, E4 5LN
T: +44 (0)20 8986 4854
F: +44 (0)20 8533 5821

DISTRIBUTION US
Publishers Distribution Group Inc., 699
Washington Street, Suite 2B, Hackettstown,
NJ, 07840, USA
T: 001 (908) 813-8511
F: 001 (908) 813-8512

CONTRIBUTING
Mute welcomes contributions of all kinds. Email
<mute@metamute.org> with your ideas

You can also publish on Mute's website
[http://metamute.org]. Post news, texts, events
and comments, or upload media to the Mute
Public Library: http://pl.metamute.org

The views expressed in Mute and Metamute
are not necessarily those of the publishers or
service providers Mute is published in the UK by
Mute Publishing Ltd. and printed by OpenMute
http://openmute.org print on demand (POD)
book services in the USA and UK

Special thanks to everyone who uploaded
images to metamute.org to illustrate this issue!
See all the contributions at the Debt and Crisis
Issue image gallery:
http://metamute.org/debt-and-crisis-gallery

ISSN 1356-7748 - 261
ISBN 978-0-9554796-9-4

Mute is supported by
The Arts Council of England

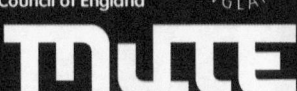

Debt and Crisis artwork credits:

Page 046 Liver (depository), 2006, Jo Pryde
Page 047 Liver (world is your ATM), 2006, Jo Pryde

Page 081 Debt Fist, 2007, John Wollaston
Page 085 Screengrabs from Net-Curtain
Nazism, Nina Zammit-Zorn
Page 086 Waste Value, Albert Duman

TABLE OF CONTENTS

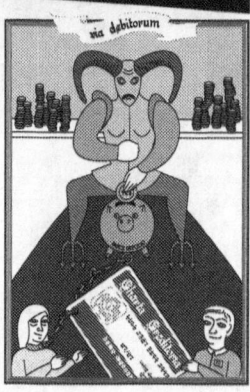
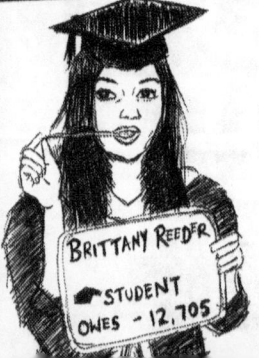

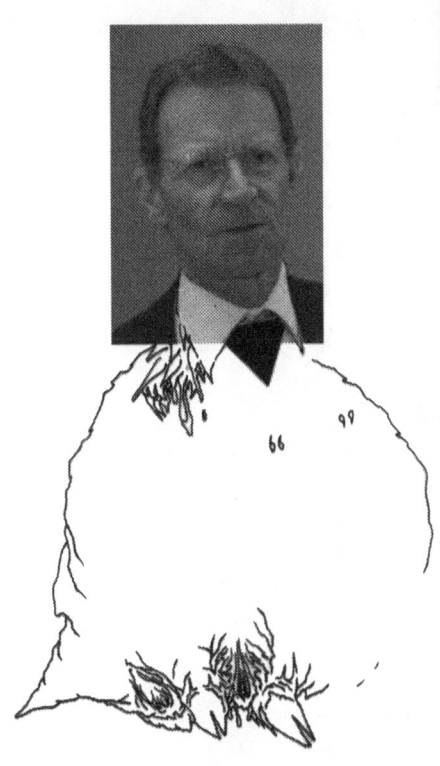

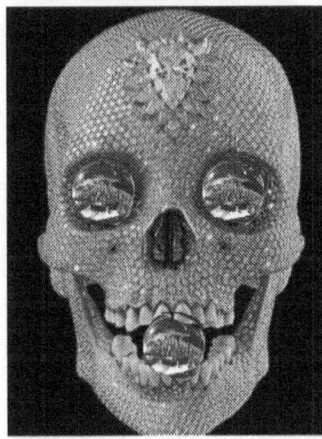

EDITORIAL

*and here are the Fascist fortresses, made with the cement
of pissoirs, here the thousand identical
luxury buildings for executives
transubstantiated with marble pediments
hard status symbols, equivalent solidities.*
- from *The Search for a Home*, Pier Paolo Pasolini

'Inverse pyramids of debt' is a useful image to mentally paste over the 'hard status symbols' of a financialised reality. When you see new shiny PFI funded hospitals and city academies; whole regenerated city quarters; multi-trillion dollar annual figures given for global mergers and takeovers in 2006; multi-billion dollar figures for leveraged buy-outs in the same year; average house prices in the UK rising by £50 a day in June 2007; £9.3 billion worth of estimated costs for the 2012 Olympics in London – just think about the debt that underlies it all. What at face value looks like a booming global economy that has successfully deferred a major recession, let alone a crash, since the early '90s (Japan/Asia) or globally since 1929, is more like a house of cards that could fall at any time.

The economy is deferring its crisis by a wing, a prayer, and a lot of looting, cheap credit, and new financial instruments. Debt is at an all time high, with cheap, easily available credit propping up ailing economies and over-inflated assets such as housing, postponing any fundamental corrections. The relationship between prices and value has never held a stable, solid equivalence – but its present non-equivalence looks very much like an inverse pyramid, with a slim pinnacle of real value overburdened by a heavy tier of paper claims made upon it. There's a lot of dollars circulating, but not a lot to guarantee their value. Welcome to the perilous world of fictitious capital.

The common wisdom, famously espoused by the US's former Fed chief Alan Greenspan, that heavily inflated asset bubbles can always be 'mopped up', and that we've moved beyond the boom and bust cycles of classical economics, is sounding less and less convincing. With the bottom falling out of the US sub-prime (i.e. high risk) mortgage market last year, and lending tightening worldwide, the high levels of liquidity (easy money) that have flooded the economy since the '80s show signs of drying up. Today, predicting economic catastrophe has ceased to be the preserve of the ultra-left, and is now a position shared by a broad spectrum of analysts from neo-Keynesian economists such as Henry Liu, to the likes of *The Daily Telegraph*'s Ambrose Evans-Pritchard. The mainstream financial press now speaks of 'meltdown' and 'global credit crunch'. Most commentators call for a variety of market reforms and regulations to limit the risks incurred through financial techniques such as the reselling of securitised debt, the heavy leveraging used by private equity companies, and the increased exposure generated when once relatively safe investment funds such as pensions now make significant allocations to hedge funds and risky futures markets.

Where Loren Goldner and Jeff Strahl, writing in this issue, fundamentally differ from these analysts is in their understanding of capitalism as fundamentally un-reformable. Although sharing some of the analysis of how the impending crash is being deferred (high levels of liquidity sustained by the non-replacement or looting of natural, social and economic resources) and how this very deferral is storing up an even worse disaster long-term, they nevertheless see this as an inherent tendency of the capitalist system. As Goldner argues, this stage of capitalist 'self-cannibalisation' is what happens when the looting or primitive accumulation outside the capitalist system (the dirty secret of its continual and necessary expansion) turns inward.

Moving from macro analyses of the geopolitical stakes of a deflation of the current bubble (the end of US hegemony?) our contributors also consider the effects of debt's structural necessity for life in general. Indebtedness, argues Brett Neilson, is no longer cause for shame but rather the entry price of citizenship. Ownership equals rights equals debt. The Committee for Radical Diplomacy consider, along related lines, how in borrowing money to pay for tuition fees students are also forced to foreclose on their dreams of the future and constrict their choices in the present. Poets in this issue explore the seep of exchange value into every pore of daily life – illustrated by what Howard Slater observes as a 'debt of sitting'. Dave Beech, James Heartfield and Suhail Malik examine culture's relationship to the economy, and question art's autonomy from the market and the state. However, the forthcoming cuts to Arts Council funding necessitated by overspend on the 2012 Olympics fail to cause a stir with our contributors. They may not affect the overall dynamism of the cultural sector immediately, but, if ideas really are our economic life-blood, these cuts arguably constitute another instance of self-cannibalisation. Maybe the Olympics will trigger a surge of national pride and enough irrational exuberance to offset any downturn, but, as Mark Saunders argues, it's certain to create a record-breaking debt.

Josephine Berry Slater
<josie@metamute.org>

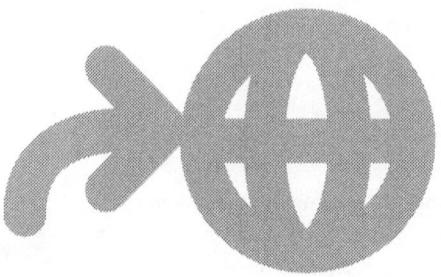

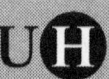

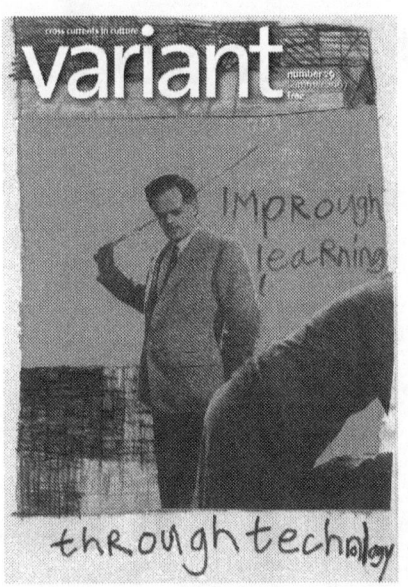

Variant magazine
Summer 2007
http://www.variant.randomstate.org

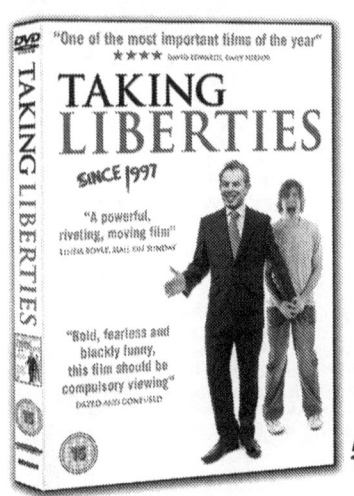

ᒍUᘓE BACK ISSUES

Mute magazine back issues
Order and prices at
metamute.org/product
or email: <subs@metamute.org>
t: +44 (0)20 7377 6949

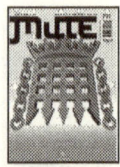

Issue 20 [date: June 2001 // 'The Digital Commons']
Including: Ted Byfield interviews maverick IP law professor James Boyle, James Flint and Hari Kunzru futurecast British countryside after foot and mouth, Monica Narula, Awadhendra Sharan and Shuddhabrata Sengupta on Sarai Centre, Jamie King investigates ICANN + John Hutnyk's Mute music special on South East Asian underground

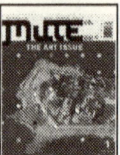

Issue 22 [date: Dec 2001 // 'The Art Issue']
Including: H2EARTH, a special project by Peter Fend/Ocean Earth, Andrew Gellatly on art sales on the net in 'Artburger', Michael Corris on the 60s notion of the 'system' and its impact on art and society + JODI 'untitled CD' special attachment

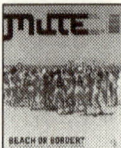

Issue 24 [date: May 2002//Beach or Border]
Including: Brian Holmes on the 'flexible personality' – a new sociological type; Florian Schneider on anti-border activism in Europe; Andrew Goffey on the politics of immunology; Felix Stalder on the future of broadband; Ulrich Gutmair on Bootlegs; JJ King on David Lynch and Phillip K. Dick

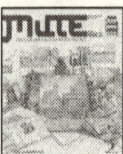

Issue 26 [date: Summer/Autumn 2003]
Including: Peter Suchin on Roland Barthes; Matt Locke on FACT; Conrad Herold on the FTAA and class war; Shuddhabrata Sengupta on Surveillance in India; Alan Toner on WSIS; Simon Ford on Gustav Metzger. The London Particular on regeneration in Hackney; Matt Fuller on *Relational Aesthetics*

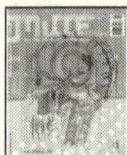

Issue 28 [date: Summer/Autumn 2004]
Including: Lutham Blissett, Richard Wright, the Melancholic Troglodytes, Kolinko, Richard Barbrook, Tiziana Terranova and Marc Bousquet, a series of reports on recent and upcoming Social Forums, Stewart Home and Roger Taylor

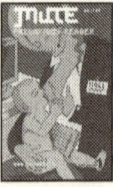

Vol II #0 The Precarious Reader
Including: Angela Mitropoulos on the use and misuse of 'precarity'; John Barker on the economic exploitation of migrants; Marina Vishmidt on art and precarity; an interview with Alex Foti of ChainWorkers; Loren Goldner on Colletif de Solidarité's inventive struggle

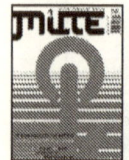

Issue 19 [date: April 2001 // 'Global System Melt Down']
Including: Hari Kunzru on the digital economy's love affair with futurecasting, Martin Conrads and Ulrich Gutmair interview Bruce Sterling on ecological activism, Benedict Seymour on regeneration in London and UK + The Mute publishing model outline 'Ceci n'est pas un magazine'

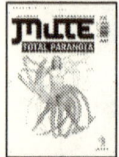

Issue 21 [date: Sept 2001 // 'Total Paranoia']
Including: Armin Medosch on Global Surveillance, Cornelia Sollfrank interviews; John Gillmore, Andy Muller-Maguhn and Rena Tagens on privacy and protection, Matthew Hyland on 'race riots' in North England, the Fallout CD anthology and HTBA + Metamute's Buckminster Fuller-inspired 'Metamap'

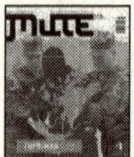

Issue 23 [date: Mar 2002]
Including: Matthew Hyland on David Blunkett's model of citizenship, Saul Albert on the Space Hijackers, Ricardo Dominguez interviewed by Coco Fusco, JJ King on peer-to-peer's attraction for the US military, Gregor Claude on the mixed message of the digital commons + Flint Michigan and Brandon La Belle on musique concrete

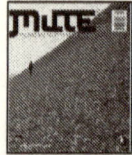

Issue 25 [date: December 2002]
Including: JJ King on the European Social Forum; Mark Crinson on Manchester's regeneration; Maria Fernandez on Documenta 11, Argentinian Stories, the Artist Placement Group interviewed, Neil Mulholland on Ambient, Kate Rich on TheyRule.net and Armin Medosch on Ars Electronica

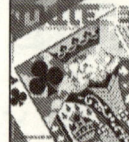

Issue 27 [date: Winter/Spring 2004]
Including: Anustup Basu on sovereign power and global information flows; The West Bank as an architectural construction by Eyal Weizman; Luciana Parisi on 'abstract sex'; the Mary Kelly project; JJ King on the impasse of political organisation in the age of 'openness'; Miria Swain on recent sci-art and its vicissitudes

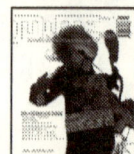

Issue 29 [date: Winter/Spring 2005]
Including: Simon Pope on locative art; George Caffentzis on peak oil; Anthony Davies on retrenchment in post-Enron business, art and activism; Mattin on improvisation; Hydrachist on the death of the Italian Disobbediente; and a special section on the politics of precarious labour

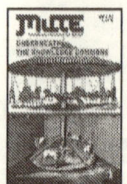

Vol II #1 Underneath the Knowledge Commons
Including: Soenke Zehle on FLOSS in Africa; Steve Wright on immaterial labour and the 'law of value'; Martin Hardie critiques FLOSS licensing; Peter Linebaugh links the English enclosures to Atlantic slavery and financial liquidity; Yuwei Lin exposes the gender gap in FLOSS development

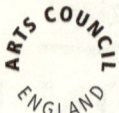

ARTS COUNCIL ENGLAND

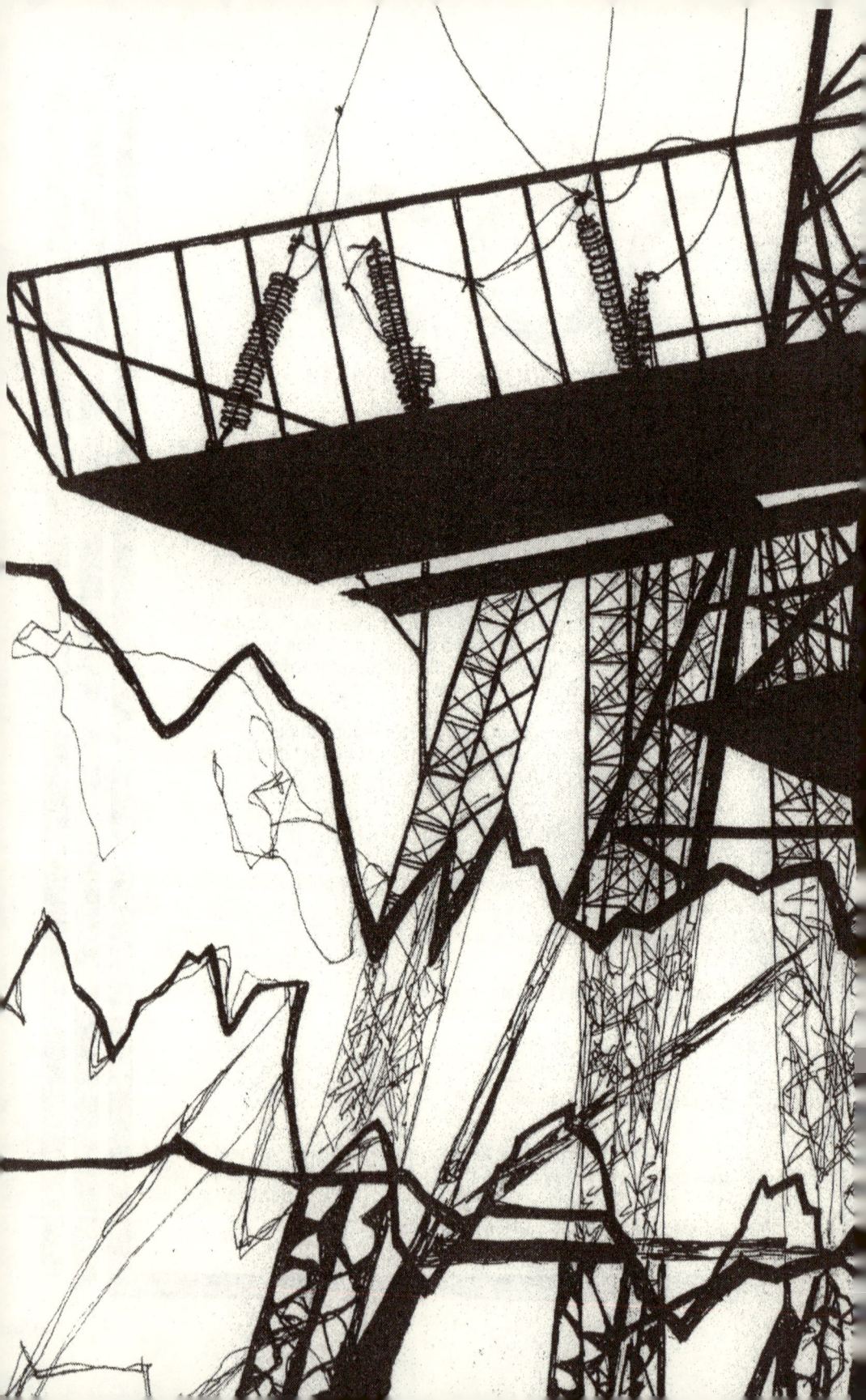

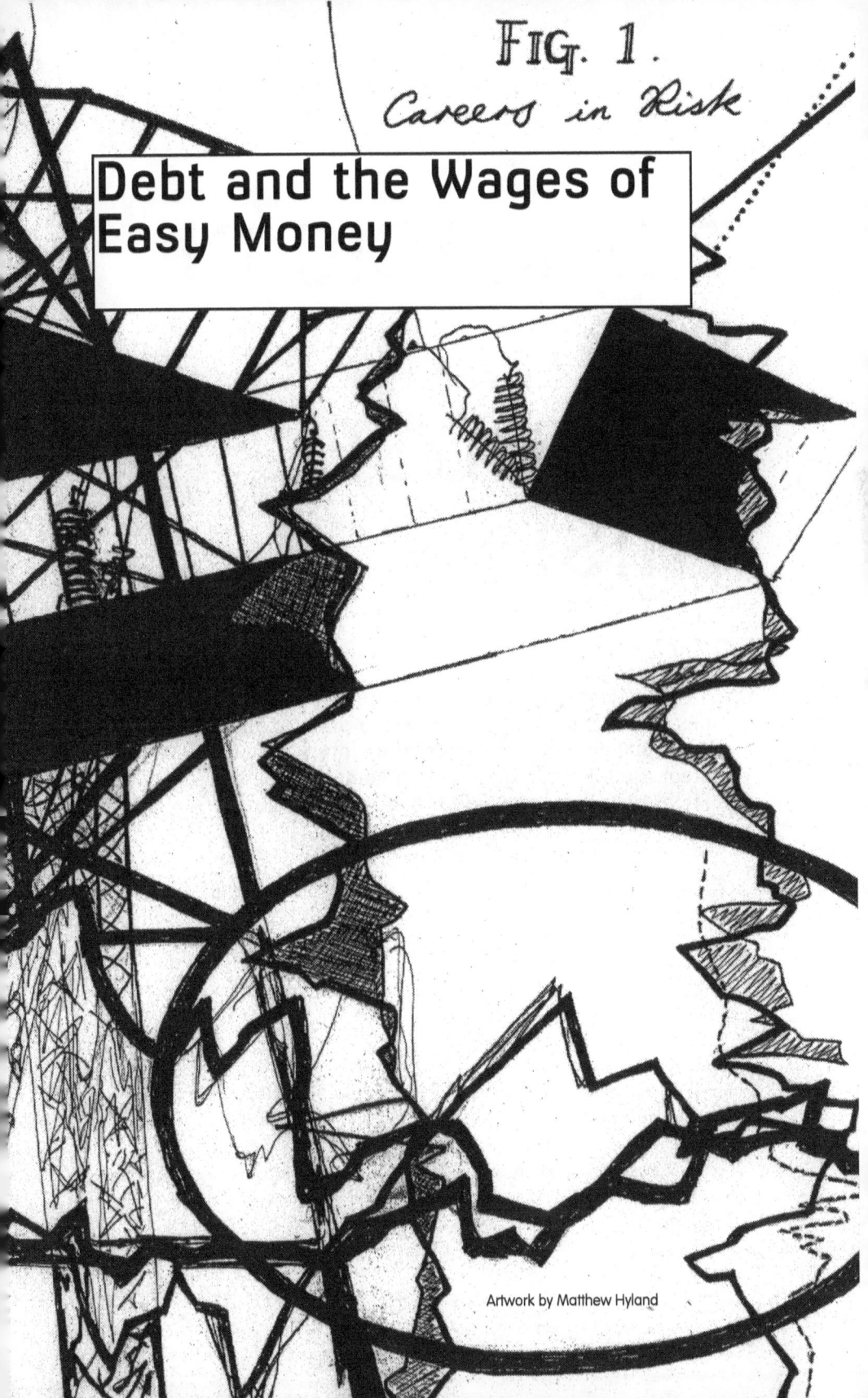

FIG. 1.

Careers in Risk

Debt and the Wages of Easy Money

Artwork by Matthew Hyland

THE MAGIC OF DEBT, OR, AMORTISE THIS!

Today we don't feel guilty about incurring debts, just the opposite – indebtedness is the entry price of being a good citizen, pulling more and more of us into the global financial system. Here <u>Brett Neilson</u> offers some philsophical and political tools for disowning a debt which can never be repaid

For Nietzsche, debt was linked to the problem of promising and forgetting. It would be a mistake to underestimate the importance of the etymological play that underlies his association of debts (*Schulden*) with guilt (*Schuld*). As is well known, the Second Essay of *On the Genealogy of Morals* argues that the feeling of guilt, of personal obligation, has its origin in the contractual relationship between creditor and debtor. 'It was here', Nietzsche writes, 'that one person first *measured himself* against another'. And he continues:

Perhaps our word 'man' (manas) still expresses something of precisely this feeling of self-satisfaction: man designated himself as the creature that measures values, evaluates and measures, as the 'valuating animal as such'.[1]

How today are we to understand these claims and Nietzsche's extension of them into arguments about the role of debt in the relations between parents and children or between man and the deity? To put the matter bluntly, in today's highly abstracted global

Images: Via Debitorum – Stations of the Debt by Chiara Birattari and Zoe Romano. Website: http://cartomanzia.precaria.org.

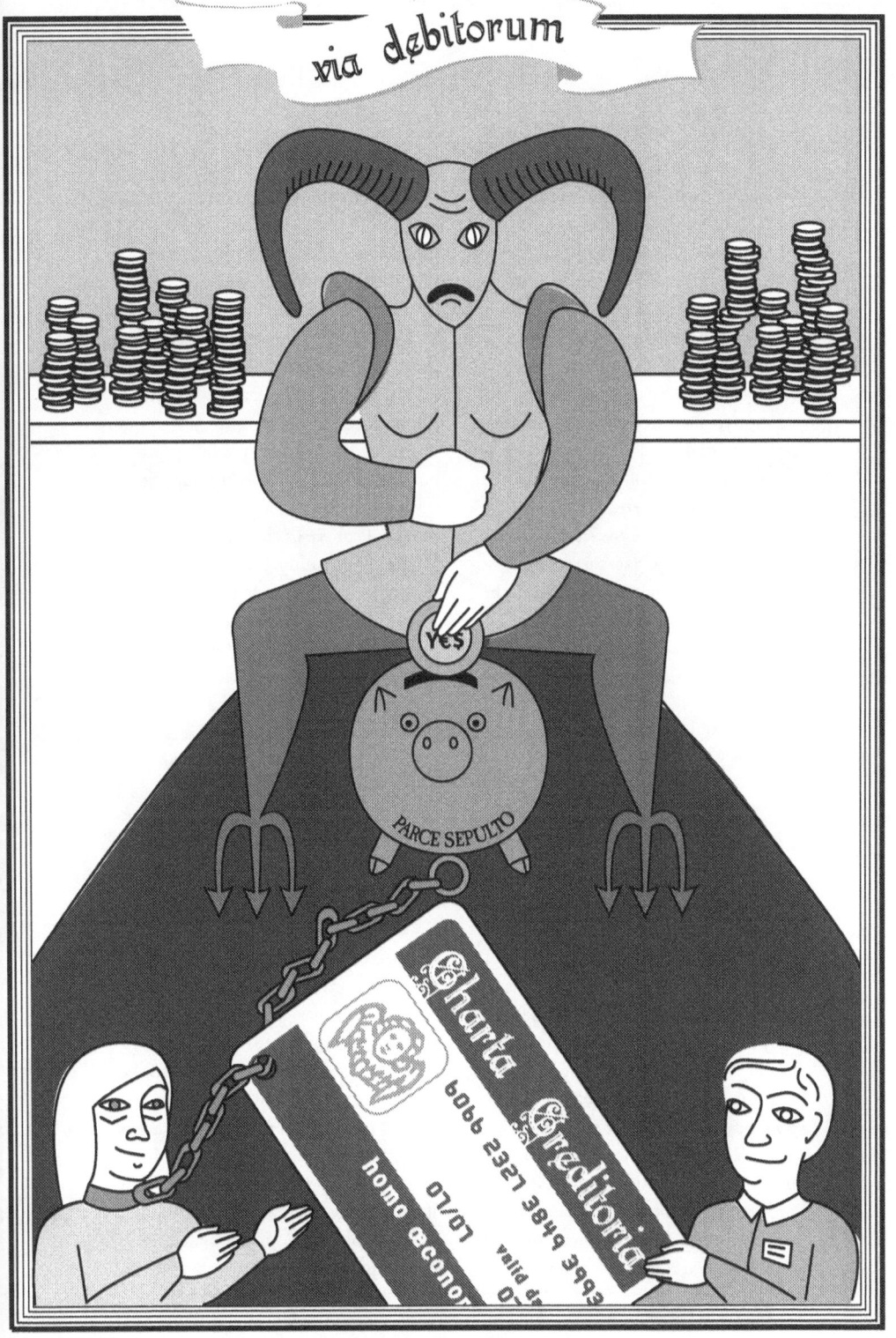

Translation: parce sepulto – spare who is buried

Brett Neilson

economy, the link between debt and guilt has been broken. Or more precisely, with the emergence of debt as a structural necessity in the lives of most people around the world, the relation between debt and guilt has been reversed. In the context of credit ratings, negative gearing, hedge funds and micro-credit, one is guilty if one is not in debt!

This is not simply a matter of social control, although certainly the will-to-indebtedness inserts the subject in a complex matrix of databases. Debt and payback, borrowing and amortisation, also imply a certain rhythm, an obsessive sequencing that measures itself against the pace of life. 'The rate of interest', as economist John R. Hicks wrote, 'is the price of time'.[2] Nobody ever hears the death (*mort*) in mortgage, but surely it is there.

To say that debt inheres in life is not merely to repeat the current biopolitical orthodoxies. 'From the moment I was born/I opened my eyes/I reached for my credit card'.[3] The opening lines from The Gang of Four's 1982 track 'Capital (It Fails Us Now)' make us realise that our dependency on debt has only deepened since 1958, when, in a classic article, Paul Samuelson declared that the social state only balances its books by 'a draft on the yet-unborn'.[4] Now debt has become the dominant mode of subjectivity, even in its pre-oedipal or anti-oedipal moments.

The retreat from the social state has only extended the draft on the yet-unborn. Non-reproduction of infrastructures, selling off of public assets, even selling future returns on government loans to the private sector: all are means of selling the future to pay for the present. Indeed, the market for the future has become perhaps the most abstracted and self-referential of all financial systems, with speculative instruments, such as derivatives, punctuating the temporality implicit in their underlying assets to create a meta-temporal sphere of circulation in which the risk of anything, bar catastrophe, can supposedly be managed.

Let us call it the post-Fordist moment, the moment of the full sovereignty of global finance capital: that is the time in which the 'enchanter's wand' of debt, to recall a phrase from Marx's chapter on 'So-Called Primitive Accumulation', casts a spell that converts the un-bankable into the pre-bankable. Debt spreads its blanket, incorporating ever more subjects into the abstraction of the global financial system. The devices of micro-credit, for instance, register the uneven but universal spectrum of debt. Everyone can have it. But the post-Fordist moment is not only that of global financial expansion. It is also the moment in which debt attempts to conjure away labour as the wellspring of value, allowing value to enter, as Marx would write elsewhere in *Capital* Vol.1, 'into a private relation with itself'.[5]

To think of man as the 'valuating animal' is to add a transhistorical sense to this moment. For Nietzsche, who more famously defined man as the 'incomplete animal', this is at once a measure of despair and a call for 'an instinctive creation and imposition of forms'. It is not a matter of positing a political essence to man, the zoon politikon, and then declaring this figure to have been defeated by homo economicus. The 'legal conditions' that seal the contractual relationship between debtor and creditor, Nietzsche basis of legitimacy, measured out by so many polls and rating scales, often seeking to measure the quality of life (which is really nothing other than the secularised version of the sanctity of life)? Under these circumstances, it is necessary to ask again what debt accomplishes, what it does. And again it is Marx who describes most accurately the magic of debt.

As with the stroke of an enchanter's wand, it endows barren money with the

The magic of debt is to make labour, the wellspring of value, disappear

explains, 'can never be other than exceptional conditions'. This is because a legal order thought of as sovereign and universal' serves 'not as a means in the struggle between power complexes but as a means of preventing all struggle in general'. The contract model of exchange is essentially 'hostile to life', an 'attempt to assassinate the future of man', and thus a 'secret path to nothingness.'[6]

What then becomes of struggle at the present time in which the legal order can no longer establish itself as sovereign, even under exceptional conditions? How to situate debt at a time in which 'public opinion' and notions of the ethically right replace formal law and its institutions as the power of breeding and thus turns it into capital, without the necessity of its exposing itself to the troubles and risks inseparable from its employment in industry or even in usury.[7]

It is significant that Marx makes these observations about debt in the context of his analysis of primitive accumulation. At stake here is not simply the matter of credit being drawn from unpaid labour, theft, colonisation and so on. Nor is it the whole question of accumulated money capital being used for industrial investment, which he had dealt with in his earlier criticisms of the French Crédit control today – the institution of public debt. Capitalists loan money to the state to finance expenses over and above state

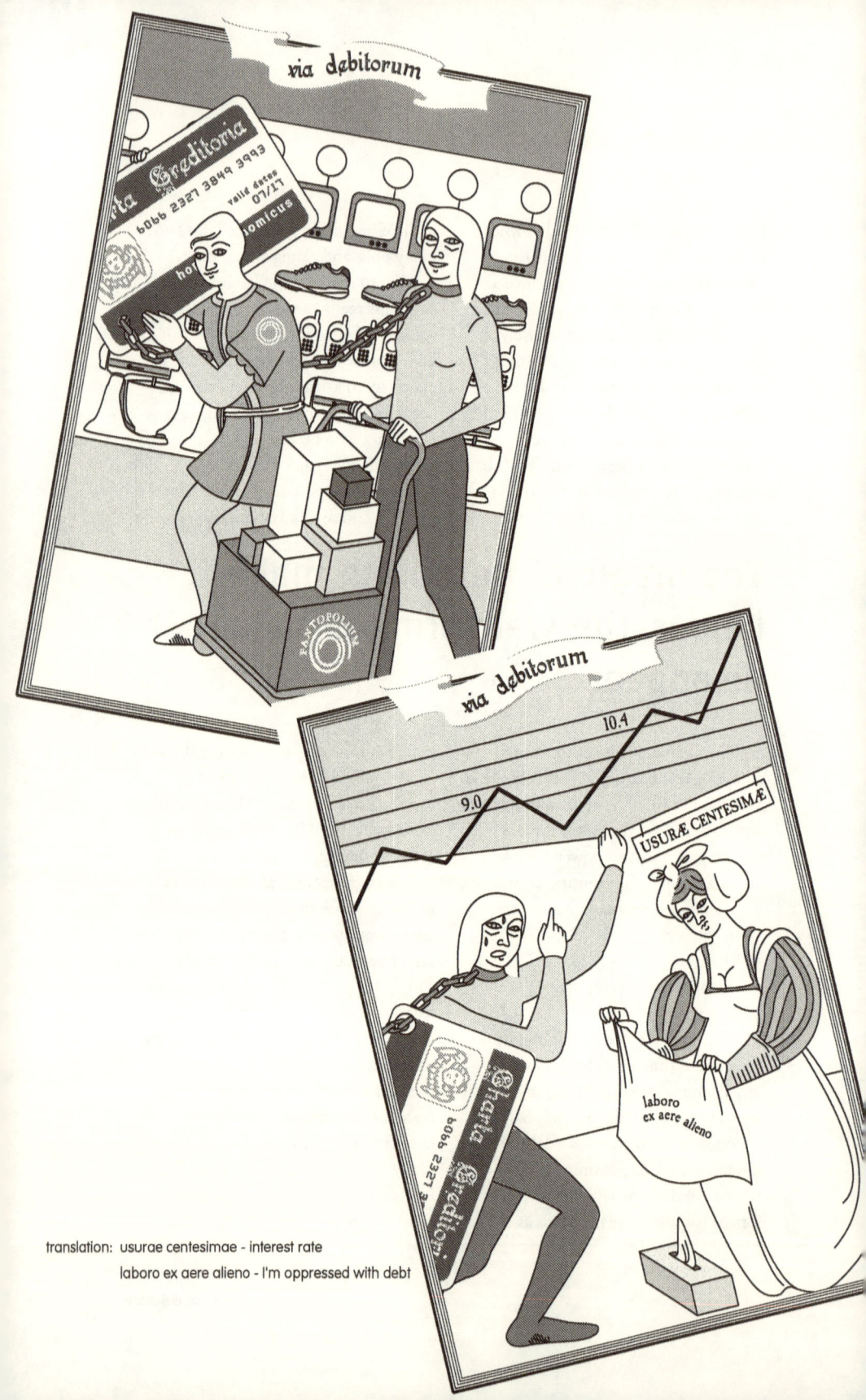

translation: usurae centesimae - interest rate
laboro ex aere alieno - I'm oppressed with debt

Nietzsche diagnosed Christian sacrifice as God 'making a payment to Himself'

revenues and then the state pays back the money at interest with new money acquired through taxation. The point is that money is turned into capital by augmenting itself, and, in this sense, the process of accumulation by means of debt is not analysed that much in the rest of *Capital*.

The magic of debt is to make labour disappear. It is here that the analysis of debt must begin and end, particularly in the context of current finance capital. At stake is not only the issue of the so-called debt crisis, created by the making of international loans to the governments of poor countries, which can only finance repayments by borrowing more when interest rates go up or exchange rates are unfavourable. Nor is the question solely about what Michael Hudson has called 'super imperialism' – the process by which the United States has maintained its global economic power by becoming indebted to foreign nations, which are then compelled to keep US treasury bills in their central banks.[8] These are crucial matters that shape much of the world's economic activity through debt. But they do not capture the magic of debt,

its capacity to perform vanishing tricks, most specifically on the living labour that drives this same global economy.

This is where the inherence of debt in life meets the abstract functioning of contemporary finance capitalism – in the fiction of value without labour. In the classic Fordist economy, it was the value of fixed capital (e.g. factory machinery) that could not be generated by labour, or, at least, that part of the value of fixed capital consumed in the process of production could not be created by the living labour engaged in this same productive activity. This is why Marx claimed that the amortisation of fixed capital could not be explained by the labour theory of value. If this were the case, he surmised, the value of such fixed capital would have to be produced twice: first, when it was initially produced (in the factory manufacturing the factory machinery that would itself become fixed capital); and second, during its use in the manufacturing process. Fixed capital must thus be approached by the capitalist as an effective debt. As it is incapable of producing surplus value through the production process during which its own value is consumed, it becomes a cost to be amortised as quickly as possible.

As Christian Marazzi argues, with the advent of post-Fordism, the place of the machine as fixed capital in the factory has been substituted with the worker's body itself:

> The dematerialisation of fixed capital and service-products has as its concrete correspondent the 'putting to work' of human faculties such as the linguistic-communicative and relational capacities, the competencies and contacts acquired in the workplace and, above all, those accumulated in the non-work environment (knowledge, emotions, versatility, reactivity, etc.) – in short, the combination of human faculties, which interacting with autonomised and informatised systems of production, are directly productive of value-added. In the model of the 'production of man through man', fixed capital, if it disappears in its material and fixed form, reappears in the mobile and fluid form of the living. [my translation][9]

It is in this mobile and living form that debt inheres. As fixed capital, the body of the worker is a cost to be amortised as quickly as possible. Thus, while in Fordism, the state or the firm would step in to assist in the maintenance of the worker's body (through health benefits, educations, pensions, housing and the like), in post-Fordism, these costs are devolved as much as possible to the worker, who must provide for him or herself in the context of a globalised marketplace. Hence, for instance, the shift from state-funded to market-driven pensions – with the accompanying fantasy of generating income for later life driving all sorts of financial manipulations, including the taking on of debt for investment in risky assets or conversely the drawing back on pension funds to shoulder the debt burden generated by housing and other investments.

To register the centrality of debt to these developments is in no way to license nostalgia for the social state. Rather it is to mark the necessity of critically analysing these moments, to confront and act on the present with all its contingencies. For Werner Hamacher, the 'lapidary' contraction of Marx's general formula for value, $(M - C - M')$ money begets commodities beget more money, to $(M - M')$ money begets more money, achieved through the magic of debt, generates the formula of an 'automatic subject' which, like the 'generation of God out of nothing', betrays 'capital's faith in capital itself'.[10] In this reading, which follows Nietzsche's diagnosis of the Christian sacrifice as God making a 'payment to Himself', there emerges the horizon of a *maxima culpa*, a debt that can never be repaid.

There is something in this moment of reversal, in which, to recall

Nietzsche's words again, 'the creditor sacrifices himself for his debtor', that registers the current realignment of debt and guilt in global finance capitalism. Yet the notion of a *maxima culpa*, guilt before God, does not capture the current absolution of debt from guilt. For what is unbearable about debt is certainly not that it can't be repaid. Today, debt has no original sin. Instead of a *maxima culpa*, we face what might be called the *minima moralia* of debt. Loans are assumed not with the intention to repay but to refinance. Only the debt that cannot and will not be acquitted absolves us.

Thus, the good citizen, whether he or she is an individual in a nation-state or a nation-state in the so-called 'international community', is an indebted subject. Indeed, debt insinuates itself in the very oscillation between citizen and subject. Consider, for instance, the April 2005 proposal of the Australian Prime Minister, who suggested that the problems of health and squalor in indigenous communities might be redressed by obliging Aboriginals to take out mortgages for homeownership:

> I certainly believe that all Australians should be able to aspire to owning their own home and having their own business; having title to something is the key to your sense of individuality, it's the key to your capacity to achieve, and to care for your family and I don't believe

that indigenous Australians should be treated differently in this respect.[11]

Debt here is the basis not only of individuality but also of citizenship, something that 'all Australians should be able to aspire to'. And, in this sense, debt also imposes a kind of border, controlled by the device of the credit rating, which importantly is heightened not through the avoidance or refusal of debt but rather through the faithful repayment of that which will never be repaid. To cross the border established by debt, to bear the unbearability of debt, is to become a full member of the polity. To be in debt is not necessarily to own, but it is to belong.

'It is even part of my good fortune not to be a home owner', wrote Nietzsche in *The Gay Science*.[12] Adorno remembers this in *Minima Moralia*:

> Today we should have to add: it is part of morality not to be at home in one's home'.[13]

In the current moment of financialisation, it is perhaps necessary to go beyond this ethical preoccupation. Today we should have to add: it is part of politics not to be at home in the oikos. It is not a matter of finding the great outside to debt, as if one could heed Nietzsche's injunction to exist beyond, above or untouched by debt. Rather it is a matter of living despite debt – of refusing its time, its subjectivation, its measure. And this means unmasking the magic of debt, its smoke and mirrors. It means the invention of a politics in which labour reappears.

FOOTNOTES

1

Friedrich Nietzsche, *On the Genealogy of Morals and Ecce Homo*, New York: Vintage Books, 1969, p.70.

2

John R. Hicks, *Value and Capital*, Oxford: Clarendon Press, 1939.

3

Gang of Four, 'Capital (It Fails Us Now)', *Another Day, Another Dollar*, Warner, 1982.

4

Paul Samuelson, 'An Exact Consumption-Loan Model of Interest With or Without the Social Contrivance of Money', *The Journal of Political Economy* 66, 1958, p.480.

5

Karl Marx, *Capital* Vol 1, Chicago: Charles H. Kerr and Co, 1906. Available from: http://www.econlib.org/library/YPDBooks/Marx/mrxCpA4.html

6

Friedrich Nietzsche, *On the Genealogy of Morals and Ecce Homo*, New York: Vintage Books, 1969, p.76.

7

Karl Marx, op. cit., chapter 31:

http://www.econlib.org/library/YPDBooks/Marx/mrxCpA31.html

8

Paul Samuelson, op. cit., p.480.

9

Christian Marazzi, 'Ammortamento del corpo macchina', in Jean-Louis Lavalle et al., eds. *Reinventare il Lavoro*, Roma: Angelo Ruggieri, 2005, p.111.

10

Werner Hamacher, 'Guilt History: Benjamin's Sketch "Capitalism as History"', *Diacritics* 32, 2002, p.92.

11

John Howard, 'Doorstop Interview, Wadeye, Northern Territory', http://www.pm.gov.au/media/interview/2005/Interview1305.cfm

12

Friedrich Nietzsche, *The Gay Science*, New York: Vintage Books, 1974.

13

Theodor Adorno, *Minima Moralia: Reflections on a Damaged Life*, London: Verso, 1997, p.38-39.

Brett Neilson <brett.neilson@gmail.com> is Associate Professor of Cultural and Social Analysis at the University of Western Sydney. He is author of Free Trade in the Bermuda Triangle ... and Other Tales of Counterglobalization, University of Minnesota Press, 2004

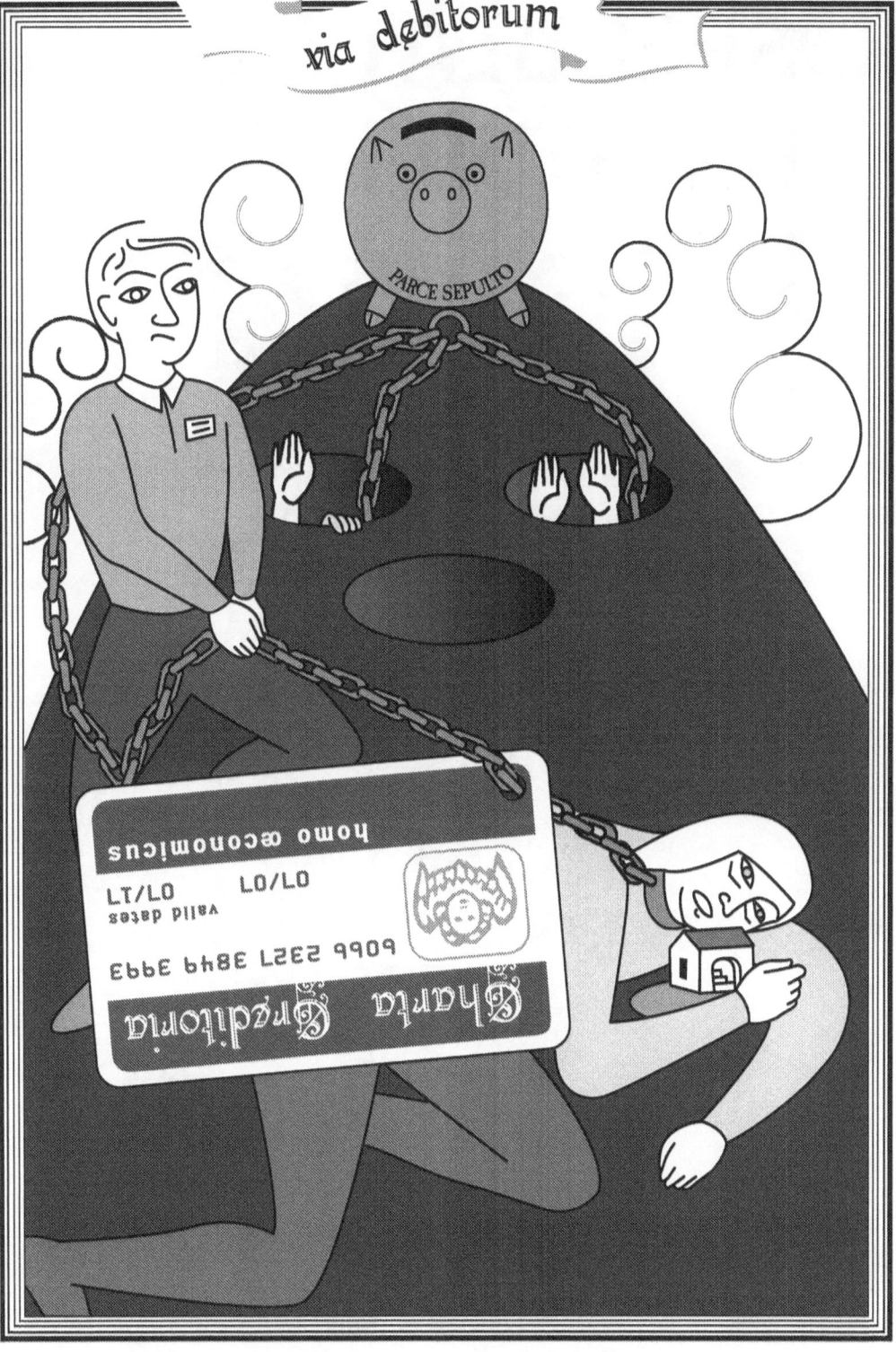

SPECULATING ON STUDENT DEBT

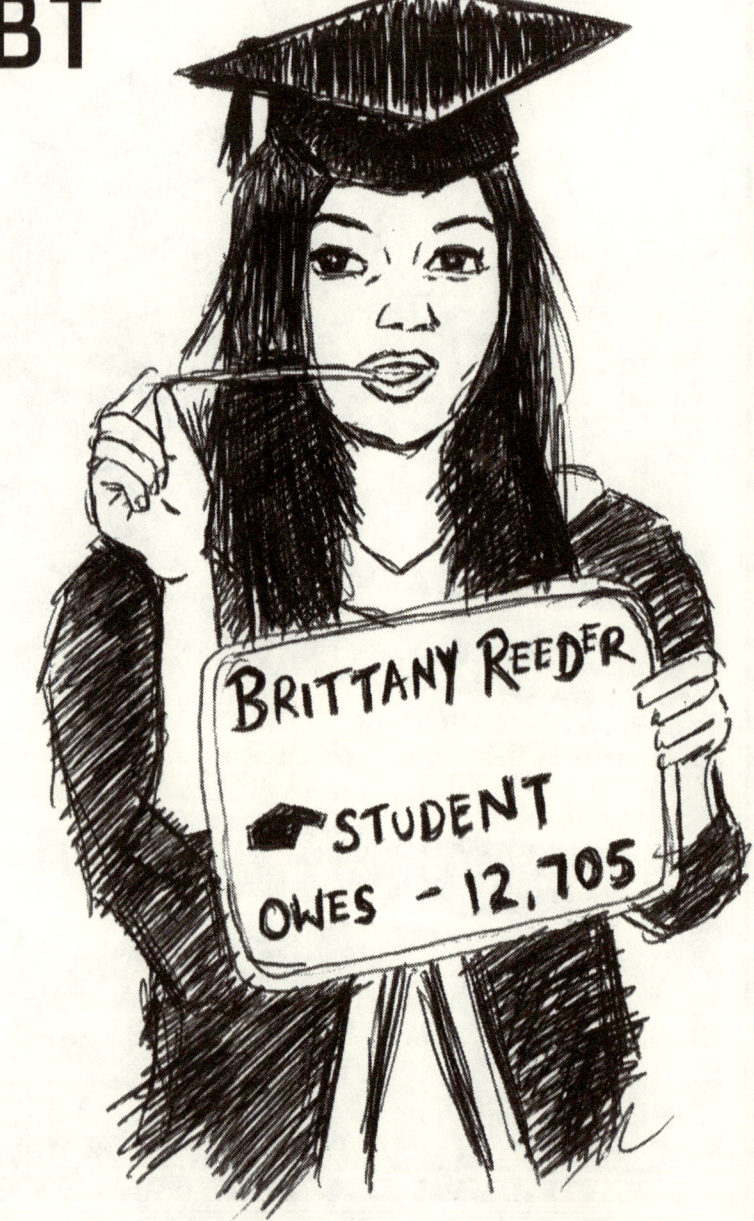

Far from being a right, British higher education in the age of top-up fees is a commodity with a hefty price tag attached. For most students, write the <u>Committee for Radical Diplomacy</u>, it offers a basic schooling in debt and recasts learning as a down-payment on a dubious future

I wake up at ten to a call from the bank, concerned that while in Berlin I withdrew cash without letting them know I would be out of the country. A text message follows stating: 'Next time, let us know so that we can protect your interests.'

Beyond late, I get on my bicycle and pedal frantically to class. I have not had time to do the reading as I spent last night working and was too wired to read the Grundrisse when I got home. (I repeat to myself, 'next time I will read, I will force myself to read. I have no business doing a PhD if I do not force myself to read.')

In class I nearly fall asleep several times. It's hot and they are clearing out asbestos from the hallway, but I try to put up my hand a few times to keep the conversation going. It's hard as the other students are tired too. So is the professor, who tells us she is in the process of ticking a thousand boxes on her AHRC grant application to get a sabbatical.

I hear about four conferences happening in the next week. I can go to none of them. I'm working. One is called 'Knowledge for Wealth Creation'. I roll my eyes.

Coffee with colleagues. Of course none of us mentions the 'f' word (finances). We talk about communes, island fantasies, this week's private views that none of us can attend and departmental gossip.

Downstairs my students drift in, looking absent minded. I wonder what motivates them, and nearly fall asleep several times. So do they. I wonder if it's because of parties or because of work, or the asbestos.

Back on the bike.

Stop at the mobile phone place to see if credit check went through for new account. I am informed that I have been declined due to bad rating. No one can tell me who decides how one gets 'bad rating' or based on what criteria. But every time you check it gets worse, they say.

In a panic I think to myself, I can't even get a mobile phone. What will I do with my life? What will I do with my life? What will I do with my life?

Off to an interview for a summer internship gig. This one's for pay, so I should probably dress up. No time.

At the interview they ask, 'what do you want to do with your life?' I give them my packaged answer (enter current ambition for appropriate job here).

Upset by yet another occasion in which I sit in the face of judgment wearing bad shoes, I stop by a café in Mile End for moral support and to say goodbye to friends – more like acquaintances – who are moving to a city with cheaper rent. That's a lie. I'm really there because they've told me a guy I've been wanting to meet who knows about a scholarship might stop by. I wait. We talk about making a television program about our lives. Who would buy it? We talk about going out on the razz – ecstasy, a rave – which we've never done in all our years as grad students. The guy never shows up.

Images: by Esiri Erheriene-Essi

<morrison55@fsmail.net> **Living in a Bubble**

The age is off its hinges
— Jacques Derrida

We begin with this short vignette of everyday student life to point out what we already know. We are Generation X, Generation Debt, Generation Fucked. Depends who you ask.

The story of privatising European education can be told as a tale that dates back to 1995, when the WTO brought into effect the progressive liberalisation of trades and services under GATS (the General Agreement on Trade in Services). Through this process education has been designated a vertical sector of the economy, which means that state subsidies for educational institutions may now be considered a hindrance to trade and thus may have to be abolished (or made accessible to foreign providers).

It is most recently under the banner of the Bologna Process that many universities have begun to champion privatisation with renewed gusto. This document, drawn up in 1999 by 29 European countries, set out to standardise higher education across the EU, and liberally deployed the language of 'inclusion' and 'mobility'. But, truth be told, the document itself did not make privatisation mandatory.

In all countries where education has been privatised, there has been an escalation from a gradually intensified demand that individual students contribute to the cost of their schooling, to lifting caps on these costs, to state managed student grants, and finally to the liberalisation of loans. As is often the case, it is the US that is leading the way with the UK following at its heels. (For nightmarish tales from the other side of the Atlantic see http://www.generationdebt.org).

Gordon Brown has recently announced that, for the second time in the matrimonial tangle of top up fees and student loans, he intends to sell off the £16 million worth of student loan debt to the private sector. The State is as usual underwriting business by selling off public assets at below market value for short term budgetary gains. The money earned from the sell off will, we are told, be put back into education. The State is also effectively doing the debt collecting for the private sector since the loan repayment will be automatically taken off former students' salaries along with their National Insurance contributions by the government.

In 1999, the last time the government sold off loan repayments, future revenue streams from student loans, administered through a non-departmental government company (Student Loans Company), they sold to Honours TD – a conglomerate of Deutsche Bank and the National Building Society. We are told by Bill Rammel, Minister of State for Lifelong Learning, Further and Higher Education, that the government received '£1 billion for the sale of student loans with a face value of £1.03 billion.' They have subsequently paid the banks subsidies of between £30 thousand and £110 thousand per year.[1]

For private companies, says the *Financial Times*, the purchase of student repayment is attractive, seen as a low risk investment (i.e. a sure thing) that can be used to secure portfolios such as pension schemes.

For those of you who have not had the pleasure of acquiring a student loan in Britain – since 2003 UK students have been eligible, after a complex qualification procedure, to go into debt with the government in order

basic slight of hand: 'short term gain at the cost of future earnings'. Like the concept of education itself, the debt becomes a promise of the future in the present. Sold. In this cheap magician's trick, education mutates from a right (secured through taxation) to a privilege (one you must pay for).

'Unreal' Living: Blasé Economics

As we are inducted into the ranks of student debtors, a percentage of our future earnings already sold to the highest bidder, we ask the question,

intangibility is a structural dimension of the financial system

to pay their tuition fees. This version of the Student Loans Programme was introduced at the same time that universities were authorised to raise top-up fees to an upper limit of £3 thousand. This directly contravened New Labour's campaign promise, made only two years earlier, not to introduce the top-up fees they had 'legislated against'.

The average debt load upon graduation is currently rated at £12.5 thousand, distributed between government student loans, bank overdrafts and parental support. Gordon Brown's elaborate laundering of student debt is in reality a rather

why are the conditions of debt so hard to register? Perhaps it is because we just don't get it. And maybe we don't get it because, in the words of 1980s Valley girls, debt is 'totally unreal'.

Debt is something that you don't smell, you don't touch and you don't feel. Your student loans go directly from the government to the university account. It is a bit like smoking: pleasure now and pain later – well, perhaps.

In a Parliamentary speech made by Phil Willis on the state of financial education, he reported on what he considers to be alarming rates of public ignorance on the subject. At a moment in which $1.3 trillion had been incurred in consumer debt (a figure above the entire GDP for Britain), 79 percent of people did not know what APR stands for, 20 percent did not understand the concept of inflation and a hilarious 50 percent did not know what '50 percent' means.[2]

This intangibility is a structural dimension of the contemporary global financial system – a system that was actually born with us, the same generation that experienced student debt for the first time. It was 1971 when the USA first 'temporarily' suspended the convertibility of the dollar into gold. Until that point convertibility guaranteed the value of the dollar as global reserve currency. Today, we are left with a reserve currency backed not by gold but by (American) debt. How do we pay debts if we no longer have 'real' money, i.e. connected to goods? According to Luca Fantacci, we simply don't.[3] Where international commerce grew from $2,000 billion worth of transactions in 1986 to $7,000 billion in 2003, international financial markets in the same period jumped from $40,000 billion dollars to $800,000 billion. This means there is currently an approximate 1:100 ratio between exchanges of concrete goods and services and exchanges of, well, money. Money is traded against other money in a spiraling, self-referential game that confounds wealth with its autistic signifier. This alchemist's trick, however, has real consequences as it

acts as a mechanism for the (re)distribution of wealth, moving value produced by those at the bottom of the financial pyramid into the hands of those at the top.

So, education is becoming a privilege. But it would be simplistic to respond by advocating state education. Our entry into the system of global finance via student debt simply confirms what Ivan Illich has always said about the function of organised schooling (as opposed to education), that it is our induction into wage relations, its hidden curriculum a rehearsal of roles in the productive chain. As Michael Aglietta has argued in his *Theory of Capitalist Regulation*, debt rests on this division of labour. While in training, we are learning to be in debt, and that being in debt means participating in the current composition of work.

For those able to attend university, the mode of production begins to mirror the speculative operations of global finance. Like theorist Paolo Virno's service sector virtuosi, student/workers endlessly perform their self-publicity, legions of Nathan Barley-esque 'self-facilitating media nodes' betting that frantic networking now will pay off in the future. In this exhausting dance of likeability, only the moderately dissociated (and heavily trust-funded) can survive. And in the differential admission game played by universities, the hot product offered to the student/consumer is precisely the possibility of access to this or that hyped network: the dangling carrot of the internship scheme.

Who Do You Want to Be Today?

Where debt for education is an incredibly effective technology of governance, in the Foucauldian sense, the affective condition of experiencing education as a privilege rather than a right can be framed in a Nietzschean way: the debtor is in a perpetual state of guilt, and the creditor is authorised to enjoy the cruelty of the punishment.

Debt produces us in a strange temporality. It strings us along. Being in debt gives us a sense of linear time, that we are making an investment in our future, that our future will compensate us proportionately.

The tense of education has taken a grammatical leap – from the utterances of the present continuous (I am studying, I am paying off my debt), to the future perfect (I will have prepared myself for full time employment. I will have paid my debt by the time I am 40). The future now.

Students, particularly those entering into the illusory promised land of the creative industries, currently experience this temporal mash up first hand. Their education does not entitle them to a future of full time waged employment. Rather the organisational make up of student life – a combination of paid employment in the service sector,

unpaid or highly flexible work in the creative sector, bank overdrafts, government loans and ongoing educational initiatives – is likely to extend well beyond the years of formal education. Graduation marks only the additional burden of debt repayment.

This creates a class of cheap and uninterested labourers that do not have identitarian or affective investments in their paid positions and won't therefore try to unionise or complain. This condition, which has often been the historical experience of the working classes, is now extended to the middle classes. Among their ranks can be heard a splitting in such vernacular assertions of the relationship between free labour and waged employment as: 'my real work' and 'the work I do for money'.

Organising in the Red

As education becomes organised around increasing levels of complexity, and working life around ever more parceled-out units of time, filled with simpler and more repetitive tasks, we are left wondering what exactly is the privilege that we purchase with student debt? Is it the opportunity to stay out of the boredom and cruelty of the working life for a bit longer?

If we were to imagine organising from the guilt, despair and panic of being in the red, perhaps we may have to start from scratch, by reformulating our desires regarding education and our expectations regarding our working and not working lives.

As Ivan Illich proposed in *The Right to Useful Unemployment*, we should seek to attain a different kind of subsistence:

The inverse of professionally certified lack, need, and poverty is modern subsistence ... the style of life that prevails in a post-industrial economy in which people have succeeded in reducing their market dependence, and have done so by protecting – by political means – a social infrastructure in which techniques and tools are used primarily to generate use-values that are unmeasured and unmeasurable by professional need-makers.

Let's take it from there.

Valeria Graziano and Janna Graham are founding members of the Committee for Radical Diplomacy <radicaldiplomacy@kein.org>. Last Autumn, together with Susan Kelly, they undertook a lay research project in cities across Europe, dispatching the question 'what can we learn from free labour?' from the back of a camper van. They are currently working with a group of students and cultural workers to develop a secret society for interns and other free labourers in London's cultural sector. Both are Ph.D. candidates and teachers at Goldsmith's University, London

Footnotes

1

Taken from a 'Written Answer' in response to Alan Simpson (MP)'s question on 3 May, 2007. Available from http://www.theyworkforyou.com

2

APR means Annual Percentage Rate, an expression of the effective interest rate that will be paid on a loan, taking into account one-time fees and standardising the way the rate is expressed, i.e. the total cost of credit to the consumer, expressed as an annual percentage of the amount of credit granted.

3

See Luca Fantacci, *Moneta: Storia di Una Istitutione Mancata*, Marsilio, 2005.

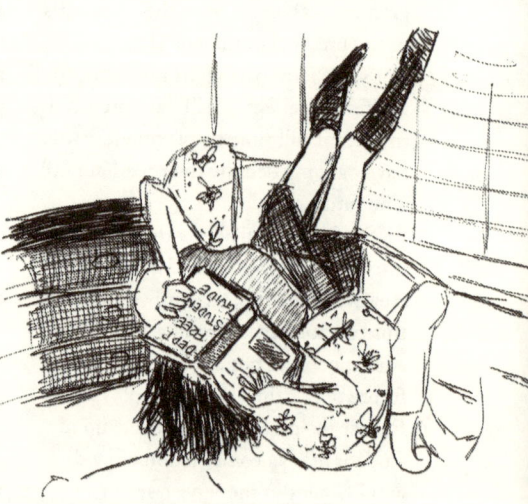

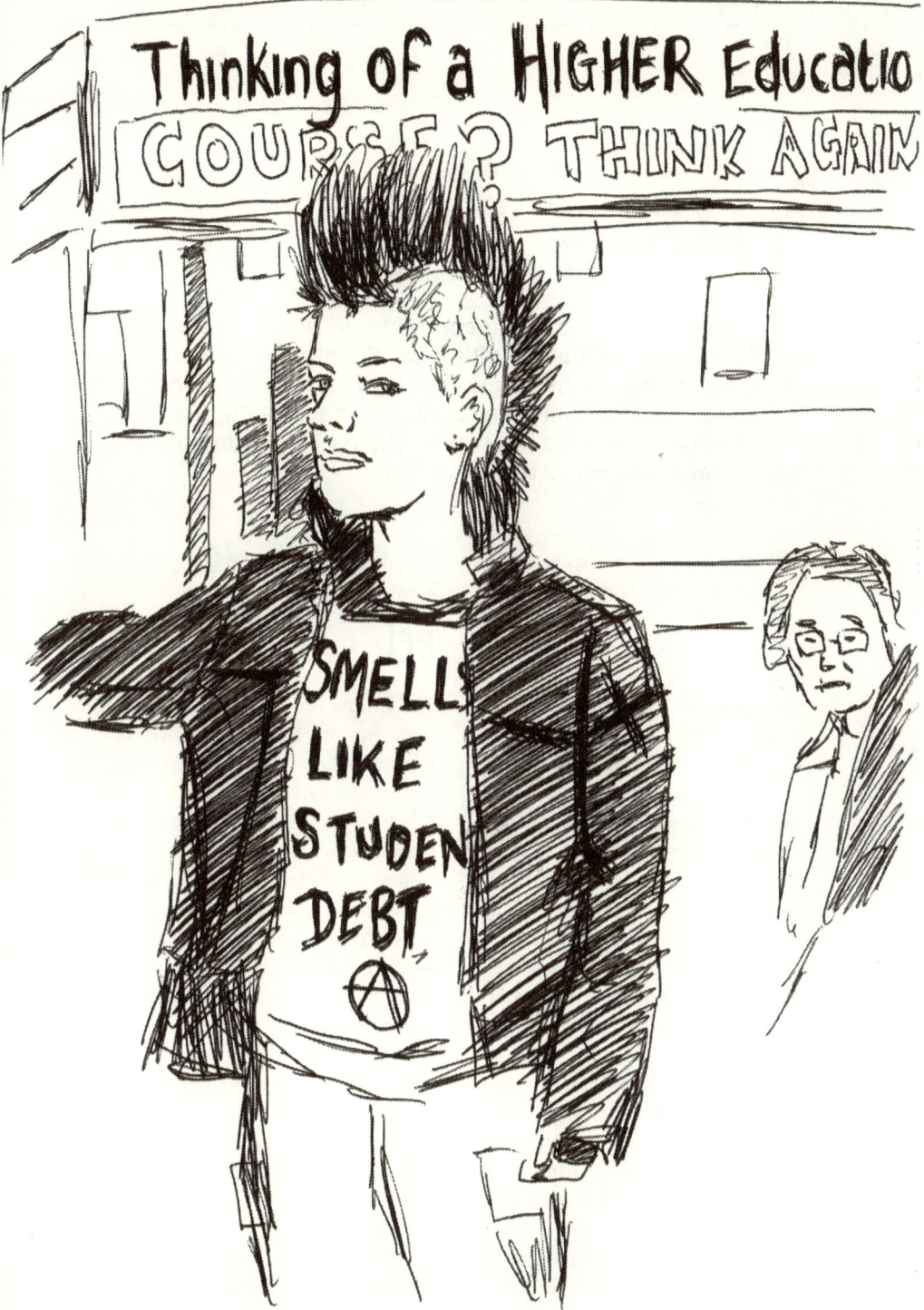

THE 3 P'S

As money expands, society contracts. In the UK the unholy trinity of Private Finance Initiatives, Private Equity and Pensions embodies this logic, turning jobs, services and infrastructure into factories for finance capital. Rob Ray explains how the 3 P's interact to pile up corporate fortunes and devolve risk on to the rest of us

I f Tony Blair's 1996 speech claiming that his government would be all about the 'Three E's – education, education, education' famously proved inaccurate, the business community has been rather more thorough with its own magic letter.

P stands for three of the most fast-moving, complex and important economic issues of this decade: Private Finance Initiatives, Private Equity and Pensions. In each case, through the tenure of New Labour, massive change has occurred, almost always to the delight of company bosses desperate to find new ways to increase their profit flows, and almost always at the expense of everyone else.

How this affects the vast majority of people is difficult to determine, simply because such huge sums are involved and invade our lives in so many ways – if you go to a hospital, leave your bins out, work, don't work, are retired, just starting to save, if you are a school child, or a driver, or take the bus, the manoeuvrings of the three P's will affect

you. As far as possible, you should know what is going on.

PFI

The Private Finance Initiative (PFI) represents one of the government's flagship policies for overhauling public services.

PFI sees the public sector make long term contracts with the private sector to provide or upgrade services rather than keeping all operations in-house. As an example, to build a new hospital, the private sector put up the initial funds, organise the building works, and agree to maintain the building. The state then pays back the money over the course of a 20-30 year period, with interest. In effect, the state is taking out mortgages or in some cases, simply renting services from the PFI companies.

PFI was launched in 1992 by the Conservatives. After a slow start, the sector gained speed, primarily in the NHS, before a series of high-profile

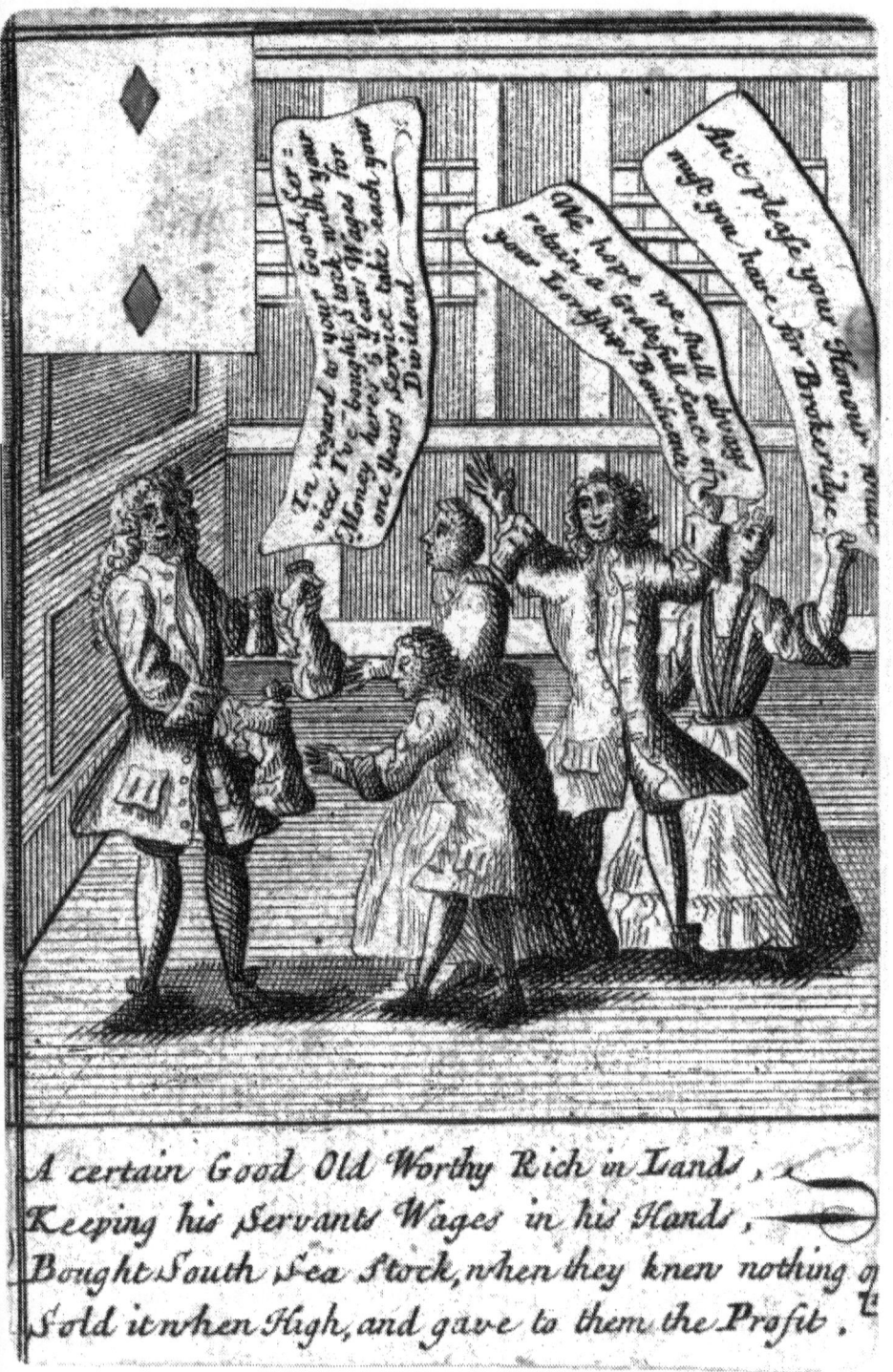

Image: South Sea Bubble Playing Card, 1721. Bancroft
Collection. A wealthy landowner has gambled
successfully with his servants' wages

Living in a Bubble

scandals saw the government forced to cut back on PFI in health in 2005, while expanding in other areas, notably education, housing and transport.

Early 2006, however, saw a reinvigoration of PFI in the health sector, heralded by the signing of a £1 billion contract for St Bartholomew's Hospital in London.

From a standing start, even with a year long health hiatus, the sector has built up a huge portfolio worth up to £60 billion in just 15 years, including over 700 projects in the UK and with more on the way. The single largest PFI project signed to date, for the Ministry of Defence, will see the Airtanker Consortium provide 14 new tankers at a cost of £13 billion – up from a £10 billion initial estimate.

Pointing to the sheer volume of building works and changes to the entire economic landscape of the UK, leading companies say that switching from state-owned to state-rented provides the only means to keep up in a fast changing world.

Loud voices have challenged this view. Unions, NGOs and political groups argue that not only is PFI a sly way to reduce the size of the public sector, but that it represents one of the largest ongoing rip-offs of public money by private concerns of the last century and serves the current government's ongoing attempt to hide massive levels of debt.

On average it costs 30 percent more to build and run services under PFI than through keeping the system in house, with several standout examples faring far worse.

The Skye Bridge PFI scheme cost £93 million when it should have only cost £15 million. The Norfolk and Norwich hospital, a flagship project for the government, saw a refinancing operation by the PFI operators saddle it with £106 million in extra liabilities to help increase profit margins.

Cumberland's Royal Infirmary saw a drop in bed numbers, poor design leading to 'bed jams', and major architectural problems after outside contractors with little knowledge of NHS needs took charge of the redesign. The cost, meanwhile was £500 million for a job which, according to one inside source, should have cost £64 million.

In one of the most notorious education deals, a PFI scheme at Balmoral High School in Northern Ireland is under investigation after it emerged the school is due to close in 2008, while its PFI continues until 2027.

This last example illustrates one of the major arguments against PFI. Deals which were signed at the height of a spending boom from the government are already proving difficult to maintain as Gordon Brown winds down state funding.

The government insists PFI is cost effective, saying it is value for money, and 88 percent of PFI projects are delivered on time and in budget, while 70 percent of state projects are late and over budget.

Yet evidence from both within and without the administration has suggested otherwise.

The Treasury itself has said that delivery on 'soft-service' (e.g. catering) commitments from PFI companies has been inadequate, while the National Audit Office has called the value for money calculation 'pseudo-scientific

government too it has enormous benefits, as only one thirtieth of what is borrowed is counted on state figures because of the extended repayment cycle, allowing Brown's figures to add up.

But tremendous extra costs for taxpayers are building in the long term. The plain fact is everything has to be

PFIs extract more in profits than they put in through work

mumbo jumbo where the financial modelling takes over from thinking'.

Most damning has been a report earlier this year into the headline 88 percent figure. In a study published in the *Public Money and Management* journal, a research team found that statistics in five studies cited to back this statement up were 'either non-existent or false'.

Two reports were based on interviews with PFI project managers, one had no comparative data at all, in a fourth, the government denied access to the information altogether, and in a fifth it was found that only three PFI schemes were tested, purposely excluding failing or bankrupt schemes and using different baselines when comparing cost changes.

At an estimated 39 percent average return on investment, rising to 58 percent in health, PFI remains a tremendously lucrative contract to sign for the private sector. For the

paid for, and New Labour have sacrificed £60 billion in public funds to a type of redevelopment project which after 15 years is continuing to draw far more out in profits than it puts in through work.

Private Equity

If you work, there is a high and increasing likelihood that you work for a private equity funded company. One in five workers in the UK are now under the control of some form of private equity, with the number set to increase as the sector becomes more powerful.

Private equity funds are most commonly known for two functions, direct investment (they are heavily involved in PFI), and takeover operations. In the first case, money is raised from investors to put into startup companies which look like they could be profitable.

Generally, this is seen as a positive thing, both by the markets and the general public. Private equity takeovers however are far more controversial. They occur when funds buy out publicly listed companies and take them off the stock market as private entities.

The most common use of this system for generating profit stems from the '70s when business tycoons developed 'the flip', where a management team takes over a company, aggressively attacks wages and jobs to 'cut away fat', then sells back to the market in a three to five year cycle.

The flip is achieved through what is known as a 'leveraged buyout' where the massive funds needed to take over large companies are loaned by banks and investors, and secured with the assets of the company being bought out.

groups and confidence dimmed due to the risks of investing during an economic downturn.

However, the rise of the 'club buyout' in the last 4-5 years, where several major funds combine to target bigger game, has recently seen some of the biggest companies in the world stalked.

A glut of available credit offered by banks has lead to increased confidence in the last few years, with the majority of the risk redistributed to reduce their liabilities should things go wrong.

Banks currently hold around a 20 percent stake in the private equity market, with 80 percent held by institutional investors – hedge funds, mutual funds, insurance companies, pensions, etc. Effectively, most of the risk for private equity is held by the

If you work, it's highly likely the company you work for is Private Equity-funded

The practice reached its first peak in the '80s when major takeovers were attempted by firms later labelled 'the asset strippers' for their practice of taking healthy companies, selling their assets, firing much of the workforce and then foisting a shell back onto the public markets.

The private equity market died down in the '90s, as mega-mergers placed many of the big players beyond the reach of even major private equity

general public, through the various 'safety net' schemes which a person signs up to in the course of their life. Paying into a pension? Home insurance? A mutual society? Well, the very wealthy people controlling your money are also the ones helping build the private equity boom by placing your funds in the hands of investment managers who may then make a risky deal to take over your workplace, fire your friends, attack your pension and destabilise the company you work for.

The sector has grown at a stunning pace, nearly doubling from £56.9 billion invested in 2004 to £108.8 billion invested last year, and an estimated £202 billion war chest for further buyouts.

Although a failed effort, Sainsbury's was a target earlier this year, and an extended battle has just been concluded with the buyout of Boots. But these are just the tip of a very large iceberg. Other major buyouts in the last few years have included the AA, Debenhams, and the largest completed so far, the energy group, TXU, for £22.5 billion.

Unions have launched an attack on the sector following a brutal fight at the AA, where unionists accused the buyers of gutting the business by selling buildings and then leasing them back, outsourcing personnel and where that wasn't possible, simply cutting staff so roadside coverage was compromised. At Debenhams, the company has posted its third profit warning after being taken public, as the company struggles to shrug off underinvestment and cuts. Unions are accusing private equity of resuming the cycle of the '80s.

The union drive looks set to be a flash in the pan, demanding only that private equity be taxed more. But the sector is a clear and present danger to workers, as a model which diverts massive assets away from wages and employment towards the ultra-rich,

producing nothing while taking larger and larger risks not with the money of the wealthy, but capital produced by millions of smaller earners who think their money is safe.

Pensions

Their, your, money is not as safe as you might think in pensions. It is dependent on a continued reasonable performance of the stock markets, underwritten, ideally, by the company employing you.

While the state works on a principle of workers paying in and then withdrawing directly from the national coffers, private sector workers in larger companies pay into 'pension pots' over the course of their employment, which companies are required to match.

Recent years have seen a series of attacks on the age at which pensions can be taken and the payout given upon retirement, using the justification that when pension pots were originally devised, it was not taken into account that people would be living longer, or have rising standards of living.

This view is a relative newcomer to the British stage. In the late '80s and early '90s Britain's pensions were known as 'the envy of the world'. They were well funded, organised and provided a reasonable living standard.

During the early stages of the Labour government however, an economic boom led to Gordon Brown giving companies 'pensions holidays', where they did not have to contribute into the pots as they had developed a massive pensions surplus in line with thriving stock markets.

These holidays proved catastrophic for the sector when a market downturn hit in the late '90s, wiping around £30 billion off the value of pension pots. Company bosses administering the pots had speculated heavily in unstable dotcom stocks, these crashed, pensions were hit hardest.

This, combined with companies attempts to either evade or undermine their duty to underwrite pension pots, has put the future of millions of people worldwide in jeopardy.

While public sector pensions have received the most attention with government attacks on the age of retirement and payouts, it is in the private sector where some of the most radical attacks have occurred. Some companies have simply ignored the build up of liabilities – the amounts they expect to pay out to retirees – but others have switched pension payouts from final salary pensions (where your payout is based on the last salary you earned at the company) to working life schemes which average out your wages across the term of your employment. Inflation, promotion and other pay rises that the average worker will have achieved are undermined by doing so, leading to lower payouts.

In some companies, pension schemes have been closed to new members, impacting the final payout for those already in as payments dry up, while others have sold off their pension schemes entirely, clearing immediate liabilities in order to release themselves from any further responsibility to the workers in the schemes.

In many cases, this has actually proven an unnecessary measure. As of this month, the approximate pension deficit – projected payout compared to funds available and being made – for private companies had dropped to a manageable £3 billion, down from £100 billion in 2003.

Some of this is due to the attacks on workers' retirement plans, but much of the liabilities have been cleared through simple growth in the stock markets. Today, newly invigorated pension pot managers are again starting to take major risks with the money, holding dodgy debts in companies which may not pay up, and investing heavily in private equity.

This largely undeclared risk is exacerbated in companies which are takeover targets for private equity. At both Sainsbury's and Boots, the deal was stalled by warnings from the pension funds that should massive debts be shifted onto the companies, pension pots would find themselves unable to function properly under the financial strain.

Amazingly, some companies are considering taking more pensions holidays, as the markets continue to defy gravity following this injection of private equity, PFI and war funding.

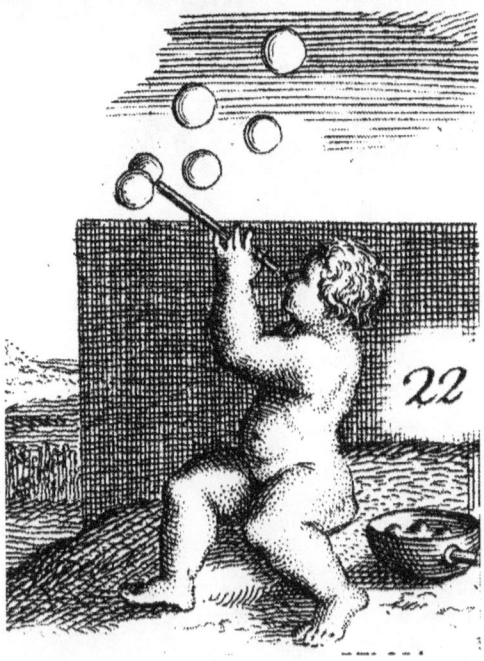

In a period of relative calm, the trouble being stored up can seem a long way away. In the financial markets however, we are seeing state and private sector bosses taking big risks with money we have earned – and hope will be there for us in years to come – to make themselves even richer than before.

Private equity is highly unstable, and a single failure with one of their shiny new multinational holdings could floor market confidence, pulling down other companies with it. That in turn would impact on the vulnerable pension pots which have invested in the sector, leading to more attacks on workers' savings or worse, insolvency and the prospect of thousands of people being thrown onto the State's tender mercies. The State, of course, could by then be having its own problems with private equity-held PFI companies.

Given the interconnectedness of the 3Ps the above scenario would have far ranging effects. The whole set of fiscal dominoes incorporating our retirements, our jobs and (the remains of) our public services, is in the hands of an industry renowned for its ruthless pursuit of a minority's profits at the majority's expense. One should not overstate the probability of such a crash. It is quite possible private equity will stumble along for a while before dying down again, in which case only limited damage will be sustained, in the same vein as the ongoing fallout from private equity today. And although the City is becoming increasingly concerned about threats to the current liquidity boom, company bosses and shareholders are always the last to feel the pain of a downturn. For the rest of us, the 3P's have already started taking their toll.

Rob Ray <robray81@gmail.com> is editor of Freedom anarchist newspaper, a fortnightly based in London

Image: Detail from 'Bubblers medley, or A sketch of the times: being Europe's memorial for the year 1720', a satire on the South Sea bubble **Living in a Bubble**

LUNCH POEMS
by Howard Slater

An ordinary ordinance day.
A bureaucratic pounding.
Not a ritual, a procedure:
dirty pieces of silver paper.

***

The zags are cut lightly into card,
spires persist,
husbands are solicitors,
torn letters are posted into sewer vents,
lift engineers order teas,
leaves are vacuumed,
a filter despairs of its plastic sheath,
lunch ends it's out to back.

***

In the square the jugglers
command the crowd.
A debt of sitting.
It's not free: the order-word
of entertainment.

***

Spoke to suicide case's father
(later re-let flat)

***

'I feel I'd wake up if I didn't have to go back to work'

***

Don't expect them to think it's not
theirs, they've paid and now they

won't let you alone for more of your
spares – surplus energies feed the line
of lingo, musty stutters grapple
for excuses as to why it's like it is,
why it's held in handbooks.

***

Discretionary explanations. A kind of
sovereignty is invested in every
officer-employee, a final word written on
a complaint form, the eviction of the
already abandoned, the conviction that
worse is to be rolled-out to the phone-dead,
ring-eyed, dry-gobbed, clocked-in advocates
of an administered social loan. Don't leave
now, worse faces you, stay, stay, stay awhile
for the edict of the new contract is
INCENTIVISATION, and Monday's report
of recommendation meets the sixty day later
ratification of an opposedless motioneering
for the sake of later expulsed sacking, lately
unperturbed to get out of here into air, the
debt of food, the idyllic retreat into some
music from the beggar's porch.

***

Gold is dead
Value is breath

***

A dark trip to the centre of nowhere;

the mill of work,
common collapse,
creditworthy traps.

Service level disagreements.

Expectant vehemence triumphs over the phone.

***

'I, Abdi Ali Noor declare hereby that I
no longer live in this ghostly house.
I am now from the mental hospital. I
have returned back all your keys. I go
back to Belgium. Bye bye London.'

***

Cabbies look in longingly.
Sunglasses. Leaden boots.
Turbulence in the mock square's corner.
Indifference is bliss.
Found people freed for an hour.

***

They'd taken me away.
But I went voluntarily.
You see, I needed food pills,
bio points and tobacco.

***

We accept euros for golfing trophies.
Narrow passage.
Emptied playground.
A tear on the brow of his cheekbone.

***

Impotent commands the worst,
usually instructed from above.
No real ground except the
communication of an order.
She is sacked in public.
She protests, seeking a rationale
other than the empty words of
the managerial chain. The reply
to her despairing request is
'stop arguing with me' and this
too is met with the delighted
sneers of her peers and colleagues.

****

Desperate right,
shot in the head
in Somalia,
in the past,
in transit,
in hospital
in temporary,
chucked out,
now he's here
at the front desk.

***

Grout case file three.
Typical foisting.
An hallucination of hearing.
Use anger directed towards
you as a shield when your words run out.
Nothing can be heard.
Audible tweets at 12pm.
I am non but eponymous.
Calls come (again).
The restricted zones of personality

disable speech, make recalcitrance.
Good morning, how may I help you?
Some gifts still to pay for.
Paladins as housing, as icing.
The language of deflection is realer,
really procedural.
Thump the table.
Pock-mocked lumpen-face eats apple.
Veer to veto (again).
Get once lost letter late.
Genocidal consumption.
Details plead to become facts.

***

'It can't go on' she says. But what
'can't go on' is not what she's here to
talk about. The 'can't go on' is beyond
my remit in this room. Does the 'can't
go on' relate to her husband's death,
the debts? Can this death-debt not go on?

***

'line line line line manager'

***

three weeks later
the same track at mother's junction
post box
pill box
snow dots of tarmac
awe of calm opinionlessness
free to be
appointed
a basket of obscure steadfastness

***

You fuckers!
You stole our language,
our scope to ad-lib,
and now you're coming
for our inflection!'
***

We are underpaid and overexposed
to their sociopathic greed – we
feed them paper and now they scream
at us. They dearly want what their
forebears taught us was useless.
They don't have the means of their greed,
the desire to want difference to morph
want, and now they stamp our idiom to debt.

***

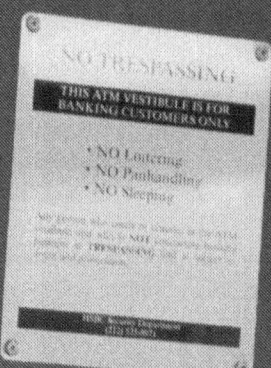

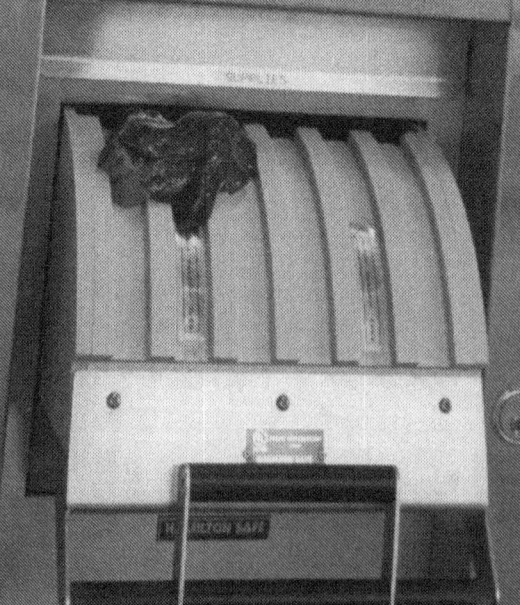

DEPOSITORY

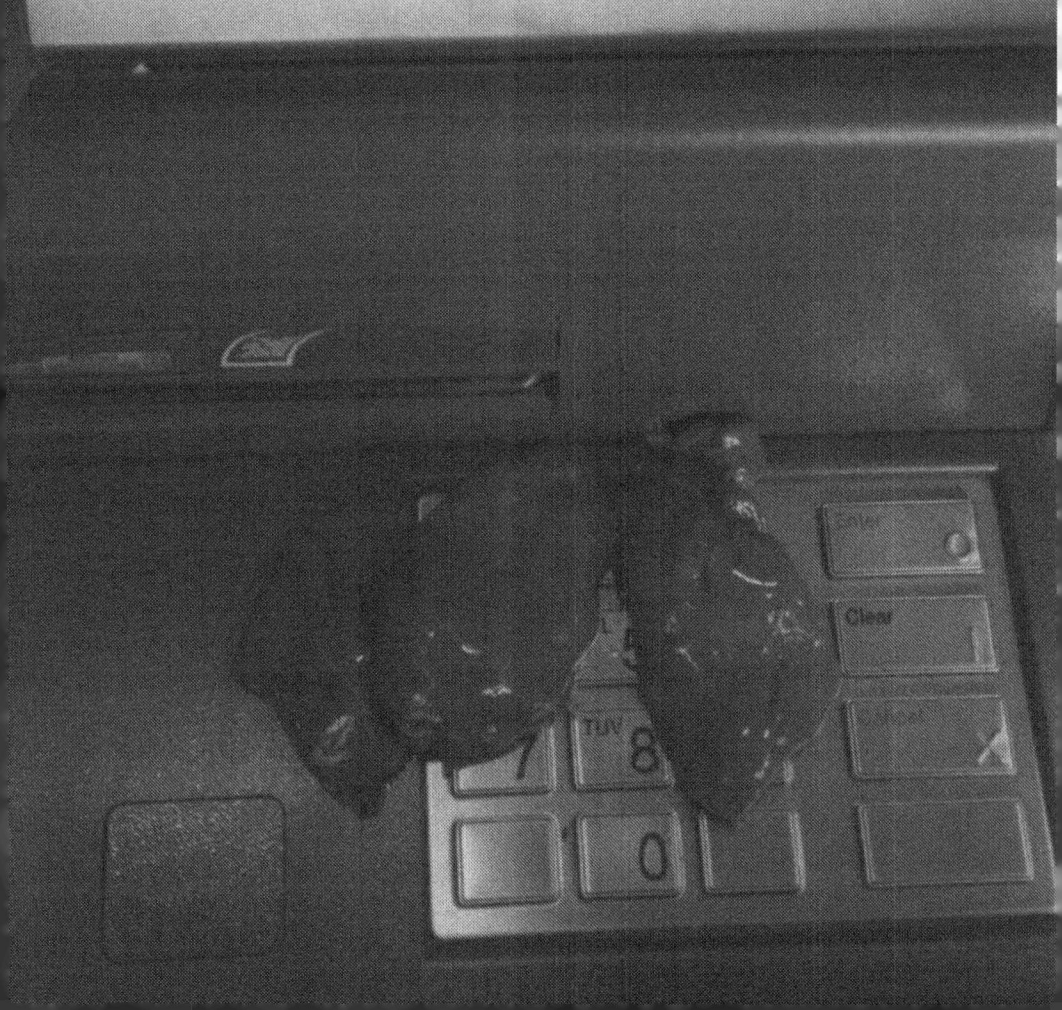

IN 77 COUNTRIE
AND TERRITORIES,
WORLD IS YOUR AI

800-975-HSBC
US.HSBC.COM

DAMAGED GOOD
by Andrea Brady

In the clearing smoke scours
the photographs, hiding the animal
labour which moves insects and their
information all over the face of the earth.
I arrive in kind by light rail
transport rough and undependable, rocking
sideways with a peg of metal to make
it ring eratogenically like spraypaint in a cylinder.
And get my tag up on the boundary stone.

Apprentice to the art of uniforms.
Off the peg on the make, blush to be
at ease among gillyflowers where I toss
suffering to be carried back by animals,
the cabbage moth, the ordinary bee.

Chances start out anthological, and are redistributed by rationing, for loss looks better
and is altogether better an ethic. I am who
ties together the navigation menu
all the compassed interests of Variety
all three corners of the fading earth.

Watch all day the screen in ratio, facing
its light and movement with more affect
and concentration than the branching
face of a lover, as these spaces slip into degrees.
Two move abreast the loan of specificity
keeping an eye on the melancholic
hourglass, poised beside the leftward arrow,
of the machine asking us to wait some more.

We share one hope, and it infuses even
the green-lipped mussel we eat sickly, the curl
of green-fringing kale. It bolts up the sky
and our assertion that there will be a future

clearing the smoke swings from its rootless peg.
That the blood will root, and take turns
through all the living work done on the earth
to divide and return to us intact. Ours is
the most abstract, and furthest from the truth.

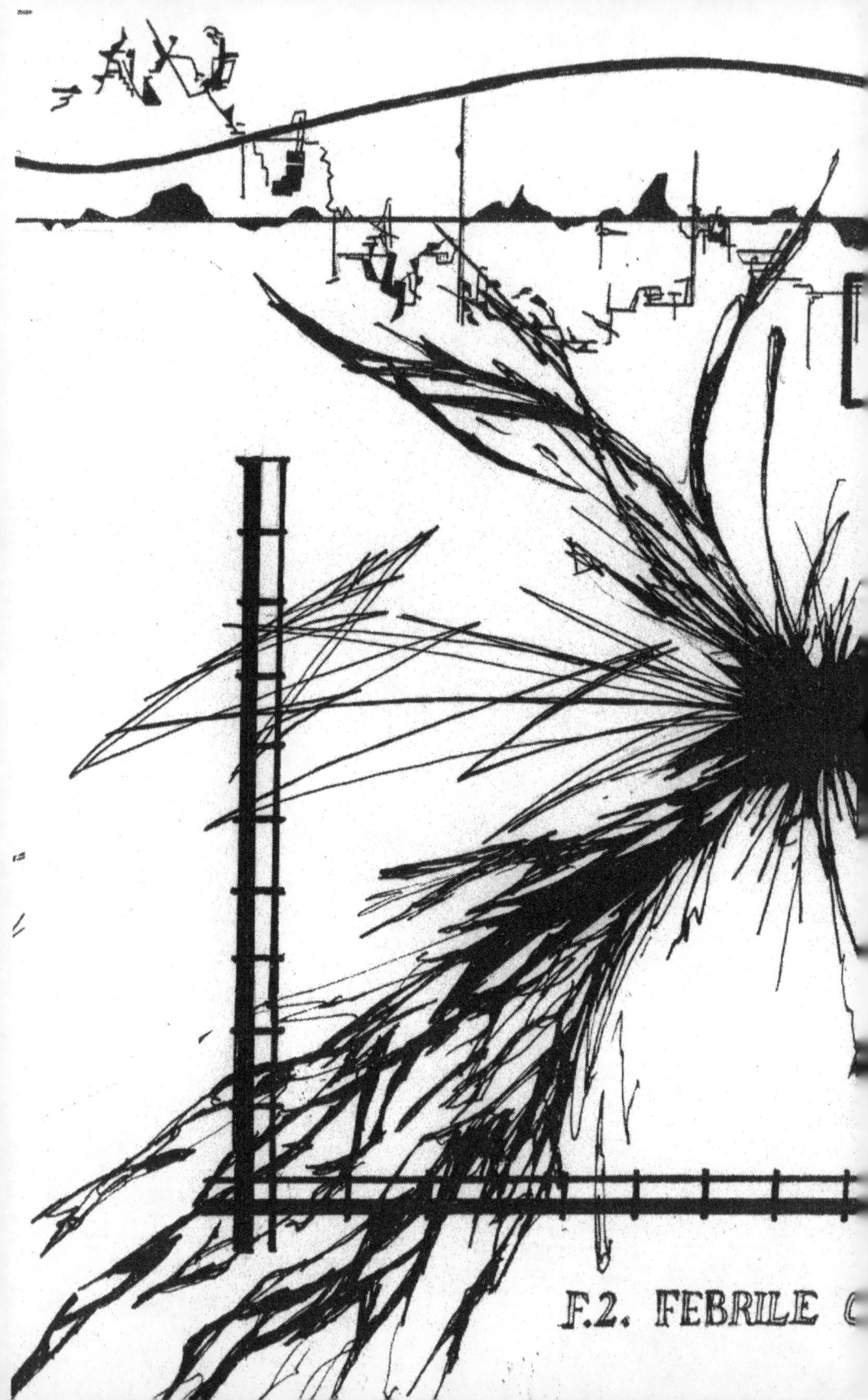

F.2. FEBRILE (

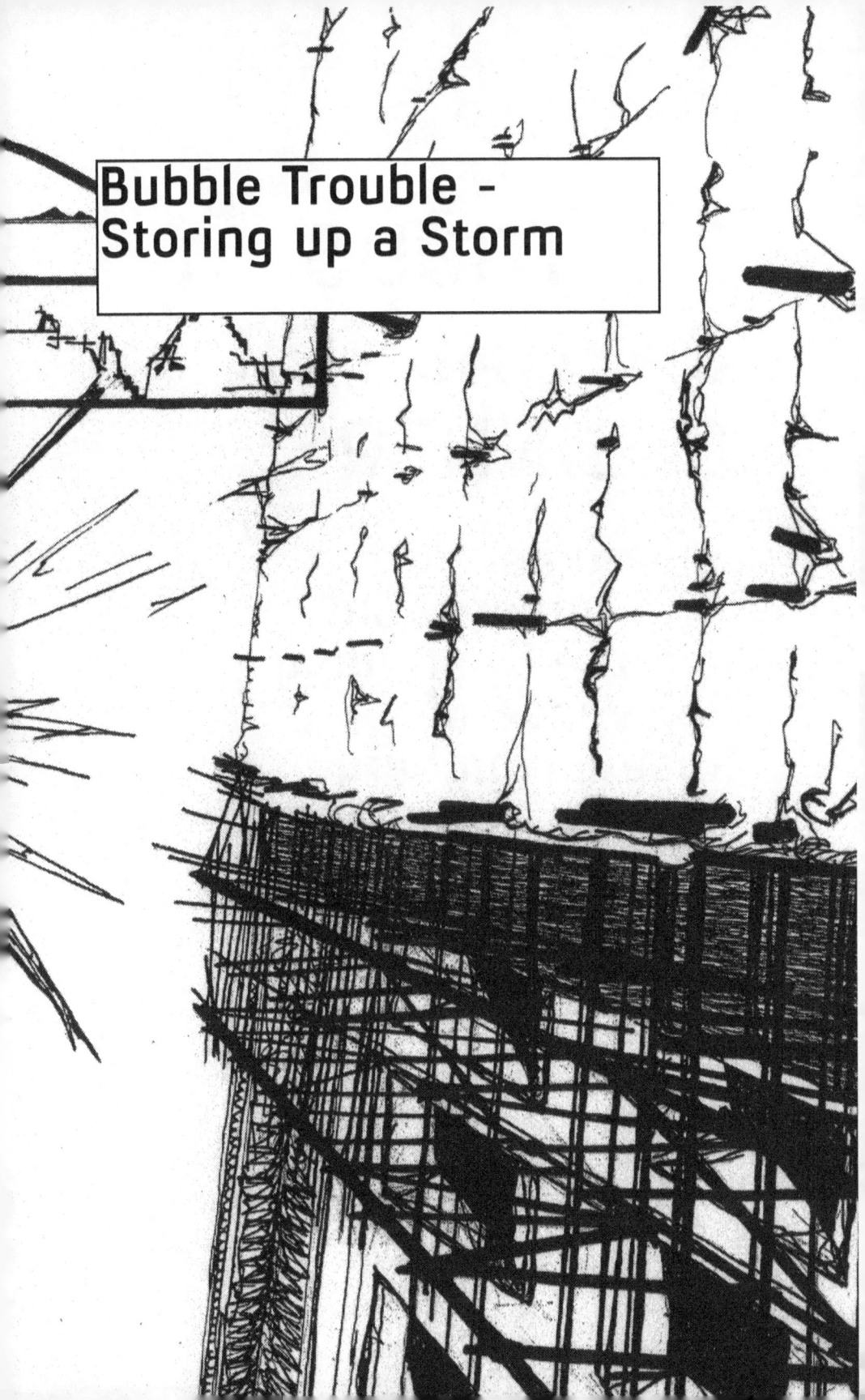

Bubble Trouble -
Storing up a Storm

FICTITIOUS CAPITAL FOR BEGINNERS:

Imperialism, 'Anti-Imperialism', and the Continuing Relevance of Rosa Luxemburg

The liquidity crisis currently wiping billions off global stock markets is just the tip of a very big iceberg. Beneath the credit crunch and incipient insolvency crisis lie the economic and political crisis of the USA's global reign, claims <u>Loren Goldner</u>. But will this mean global depression, wars and intensified authoritarianism, or a renewed opportunity for communism? Goldner returns to the theories of Marx and Luxemburg to examine today's financial and military imperialism, and its left wing 'anti-imperialist' mirror

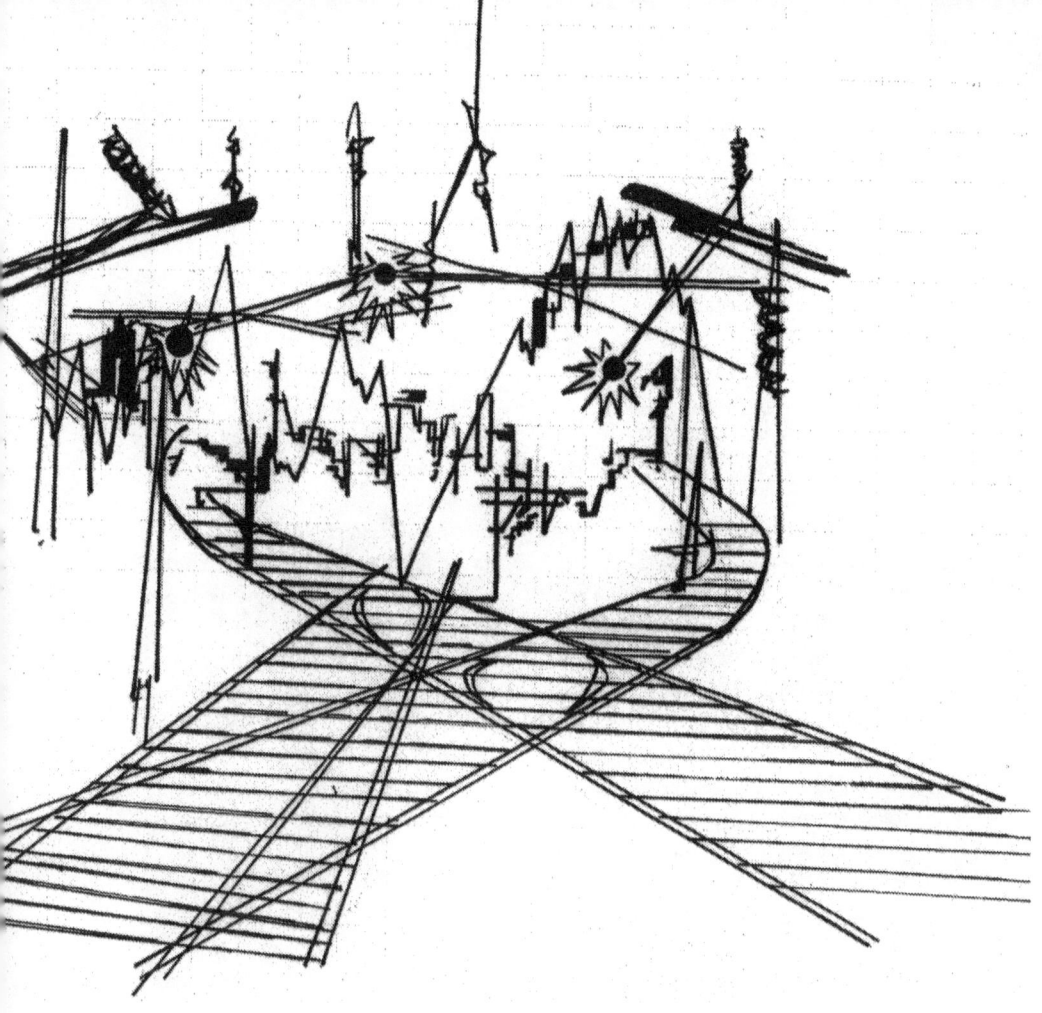

I n February of this year the Chinese stock market, which had long been suspected of being in a runaway bubble phase, took a plunge. In the following days that tremor was felt in stock markets around the world. China in recent months has reached the 'shoe shine boy' phase of popular stock speculation (a major American investor famously decided to get out of the stock market just before the 1929 crash when a shoeshine boy gave him advice on stocks), and after the (not so welcome) correction, the Chinese market resumed its upward rush to new highs, followed with relief by investors everywhere.

With the slightest historical perspective, we can see that the world shock set off by such a hiccup in a still relatively small market (in terms of what savvy people call 'total market capitalisation') is something quite new, unthinkable only a few years ago. China's stock market can have such an impact because people are aware that any pause, not to say downturn in the country's economic boom (averaging

Images: by Matthew Hyland   **Living in a Bubble**

over 10 percent GDP growth for years on end, whereas Britain in its 19th century heyday was considered quite impressive at 3 or 4 percent) could bring the contemporary worldwide financial euphoria to an end. Increasingly insiders and pundits talk openly of the 'when, not if' of a global downturn, or even (for some) cataclysm.

With a bit more historical perspective, we can recall the late 1980s myth of the Japanese economic juggernaut, when the Imperial Palace in Tokyo was briefly priced at a higher value than all the real estate in California. And we recall that juggernaut hit a wall in 1990 in a stock market and real estate meltdown that lasted some 16 years. It does not seem impossible that we will look back on a meltdown of the current Chinese juggernaut in somewhat the same way, but the consequences will be more far reaching.

These, however, are relatively surface, almost journalistic observations about phenomena arising from the real issues of how the world economy actually works, or more precisely, doesn't work for much of humanity.

In fact, what we are seeing today is just the culmination of a process underway since the late 1950s, (the proverbial 'from a scratch to the danger of gangrene'), whereby an ever-increasing mass of nomad dollars, corresponding to no real wealth in the world economy, are tossed around like a hot potato by central banks always counting on the 'bigger fool' to be

holding them when they finally deflate. The central banks of Asia (China, Japan, South Korea and Taiwan) currently hold over $2 trillion of these nomad dollars, and China alone is expected to have $2 trillion by some time in 2008.

We can call these dollars, which represent uncollectible debts arising first or all from five decades of chronic American balance-of-payments deficits, 'fictitious capital', a concept which, when unpacked, leads straight to the heart of 50 years of capitalist history and to the illumination of our own precarious present.

The following aims to show that, far from being a remote 'economic' concept, fictitious capital leads us straight to the central political questions of today, and above all those questions confronting the international left. To see this clearly, we must connect these fictitious nomad dollars to the dynamics of contemporary geopolitics and the closely related class struggle.

IMPERIALISM AND SUPER IMPERIALISM

Some 90 years ago, V.I. Lenin wrote a book, *Imperialism* (1916), which purported to explain the origins of the First World War and the abject capitulation of the socialist parties in 1914 (with a few noble exceptions) to 'social patriot' support for their own bourgeoisie in that war. Lenin

'fictitious capital' leads to the heart of 50 years of history and today's central political questions

portrayed a world economy of 'monopoly capital' and giant cartels fighting for control of the planet. But the political payoff of Lenin's analysis (quite apart from his questionable economics) was multiple: he argued that the imperialist powers (i.e. Europe and the US, and later the newly arrived Japan) were 'exporting capital' (an idea borrowed from the British Fabian Hobson) that could not be profitably invested in the capitalist heartland, and that the 'super-profits' from this capital export helped to buy off an 'aristocracy of labour' in the Western working classes, explaining the accommodation in each country of this 'aristocracy' to its respective national bourgeosie.

Lenin's little book would probably have been forgotten had he not led the Russian Revolution a year later, and helped found the Third (Communist) International in which his theses, after his death in 1924, were enshrined as writ, with repercussions extending, through the international impact of Stalinism, for decades.

Lenin had already skirmished, and generally unhappily, with a revolutionary contemporary, Rosa Luxemburg. In her *Accumulation of Capital* (1913), a work much more grounded in Marx's problematic than Lenin's pamphlet, Luxemburg argued that imperialism expressed the continuing presence of what Marx had called 'primitive accumulation', a certain increment of 'loot' which capitalism required to compensate for a disequilibrium internally generated by its dynamic. The implications of Luxemburg's analysis were that the goods and machinery capitalism was exporting to peasants and petty producers in the heartland and in the burgeoning colonial world were in fact exchanged for a huge increment of unpaid wealth (cf. her unforgettable descriptions of the looting of American farmers, African tribesmen, Egyptian and Chinese peasants), a looting that was extended to capitalism's own working class through taxation to pay for the pre-1914 arms race, driving real wages below the level required for the working class to reproduce itself. Far from constituting an aristocracy, the working class within capitalism was, for Luxemburg, increasingly subjected to a complementary form of the primitive

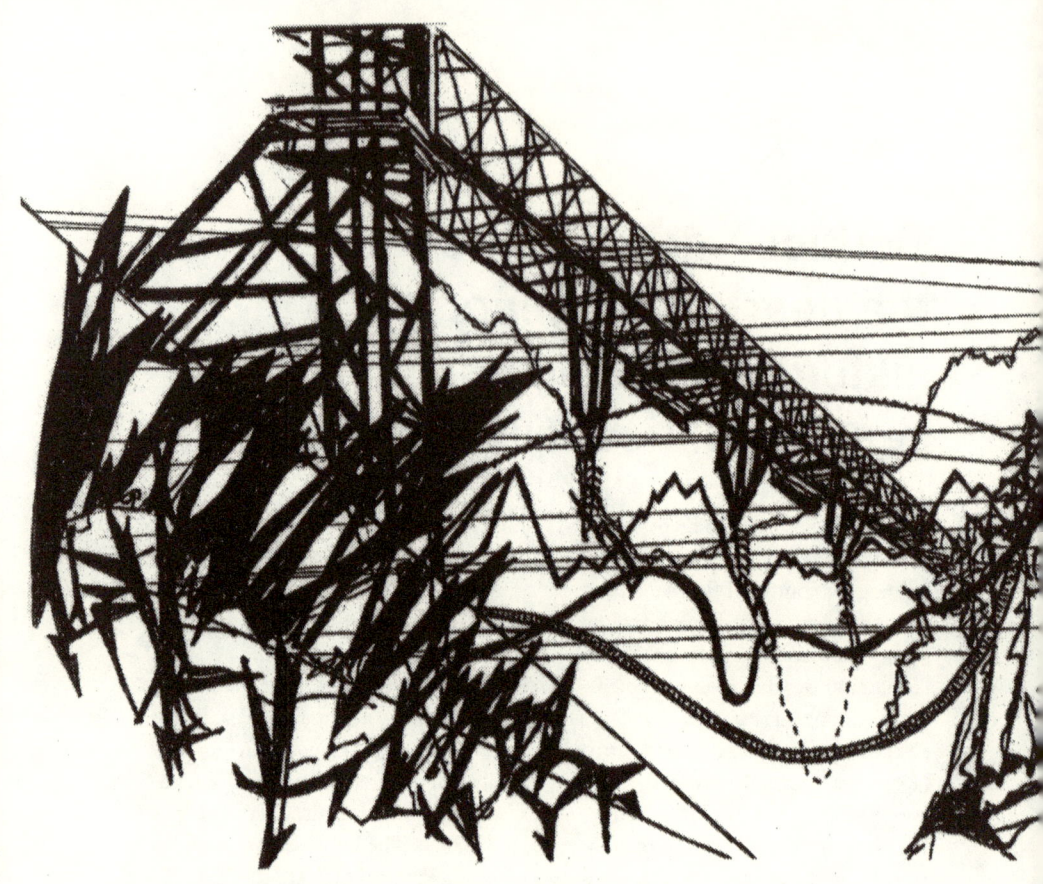

accumulation which the system visited on petty producers of the non-capitalist world. These complementary aspects, inward and outward, of 'looting' in fact anticipated the fascism which emerged in Germany and elsewhere two decades later.

I have minor differences with Luxemburg (as will be shown below) but her posing of the problem takes us much farther than Lenin's in understanding today's world.

This debate from 90 years ago is important because, despite the post-modern platitudes of figures such as Hardt and Negri, or e.g. the protestations of the much more rigorous orthodox Marxism of the school around Paolo Giussani in Italy, imperialism is still very much with us. While this might seem obvious, the serious theoretical amnesia and retrogression on the international left in the past three decades oblige us to quickly sketch some recent history. Iraq of course speaks for itself as a classical imperialist adventure. But beyond the obvious, let's begin by pointing to the US military presence, overt and covert, in 110 countries and its largely successful counter-insurgency in Latin America and the Caribbean. We can

Luxemburg argued imperialism is about 'loot' offsetting capital's internal disequilibrium

include the various 'revolutions' backed overtly or covertly by the US in Serbia, Georgia and the Ukraine (the US embassy in Kiev has 750 employees). All this is connected, once again, to a geopolitical strategy aimed at controlling the borderlands of Russia and China, a classic remake of the 19th century 'great game'. In this perspective, the US backed the extension of NATO to include most of the former Warsaw Pact states, right at Russia's doorstep. The US (sorry, I mean NATO) intervened in the wars in ex-Yugoslavia and militarily humiliated Serbia. Most recently, the US is assuring everyone that its proposed anti-missile systems in Poland and the Czech Republic pose no threat to Russia, and is pushing the independence of Kosovo against growing Russian opposition.

The US, officially and unofficially, is at the same time 'greatly concerned' about China's new presence in Africa and elsewhere in the Third World, particularly where oil is involved. Western experts have had the cheek to warn China against 'unfairly exploiting Africa's natural resources'. A great power rivalry over raw materials in Africa, Asia, and Latin America? Haven't we been here before?

In East Asia, the US maintains 35,000 troops in South Korea, important bases in (and a close alliance with) Japan, naval fleets ready to defend Taiwan, all aimed at containing what the CIA openly identified as the main future rival of the US: China. When China recently showed the world the efficacy of its new anti-satellite missiles, the US, with hundreds of nuclear warheads aimed at China, growled about the hypocrisy of China's claims to be pursuing 'peaceful emergence'.

In the Middle East, current US dominance of world oil production, a fundamental weapon in keeping potential rivals down, has dictated everything from support to the hilt for Israel to helping foment the (how short lived!) anti-Syrian 'Cedar Revolution' in Lebanon, and close ties with NATO partner Turkey as a counter-weight to Iran. The US has more military hardware in the little Gulf state of Qatar than in any other country in the world except Germany.

I have limited myself thus far mainly to the geopolitical and military level. But let's not forget the over 200 multinationals, most of them American, which still constitute the lion's share (and an increased share) of world production.

To this we can add the weight of the US through 'international' institutions such as the UN, the IMF and World Bank, the latter two imposing 'structural adjustment' programmes on 100 developing countries, producing over 60 failed or near-failed states; we can add the 'fact' that the income ratio of the West to the developing world has greatly increased in the past 30 years, in spite of important development in countries such as China, Brazil and more recently in India during that time. It is no secret that the military overreach described above is the 21st century extension of the proverbial gunboats of earlier times for the enforcement of IMF and World Bank dictats. Capital, except in 'free market' fantasy, never exists without a state and without the 'special body of armed men' (as Engels termed the military and police) who, when necessary, collect debts for the state.

Some sceptics have asked what imperialism means when a country such as China, with an average per capita income of $1,200 a year, has lent something rapidly approaching $2 trillion to the 'lone superpower', and this takes us right back to Lenin and Rosa Luxemburg.

Michael Hudson's excellent book, *Super Imperialism* (1972; new edition 2002) anticipates, and answers that question. Hudson shows that US imperialism since World War II has

not, indeed, followed Lenin's model (which was always flawed), but has perfected the strategy of 'managing empire through bankruptcy'. The $1-2 trillion in the Bank of China consists of little green pieces of paper (dollars and dollar-denominated bonds) exchanged for real Chinese goods produced by the exploitation of Chinese workers, pieces of paper then re-lent to the 'US consumer' so he/she can buy those goods. That money will never be seriously repaid, particularly if US policy makers get their way and the Chinese revalue their currency (from 7.8 renminbi = $1) to the desired level of 4 renminbi = $1, cutting in half the value of those reserves to themselves. The Japanese, who saw their dollar holdings reduced in value by Nixon's dissolution of the old Bretton Woods system in 1971, can tell the Chinese a thing or too (and the Chinese know the stakes very well and have discussed them publicly).

But the mere enumeration of the dimensions of imperialism today still does not adequately get at the dynamic of the system, both 'geopolitically' and above all in terms of the international class struggle. For what we are living through is a potential passing of the 'baton' of empire from the US to Asia, quite analogous to the shift from British to America-centred world accumulation between 1914 and 1945 (the latter being the true stakes of the wars, depressions and social upheavals of those years).

despite Hardt and Negri's post-modern platitudes, imperialism is still very much with us

We further note that just as the previous world imperial system 'cracked', just after World War I, there occurred from 1917 to 1921 the biggest revolutionary offensive in the history of the world working class, and we can say with guarded optimism that the 'cracking' of US world hegemony confronted with the rise of Asia (a transition whose success is far from assured) just might witness a still bigger working class offensive, hopefully with happier results. That, underneath all appearances, is what is at stake today, and the success of such an offensive is obviously opposed by both the declining US hegemon and by a constellation of forces from China to Latin America by way of the Taliban coalescing under the banner of 'anti-imperialism'.

Finally, just as the weakening of British (and secondarily French) world domination in the early 20th century frayed and finally broke on the 'weak link' Russia and its two (1905, 1917) revolutions, so today the fault line of the contemporary 'game for the world' lies along the borders of Russia and China from the Baltic to Korea and Japan, and it will be in the looming confrontation between Asia and the US that the future working class upsurge will emerge and either triumph or be crushed under the emergence of a new centre of world accumulation.

But to see the true dimensions of the contemporary stakes, let's get down into the 'deep' economic questions. None of the preceding would be fully intelligible without being connected to the crisis of world capitalist accumulation underway since the early 1970s.

Contemporary sceptics and willful amnesiacs who question whether imperialism has any meaning today throw Rosa Luxemburg's *Accumulation of Capital* into the same historical dustbin as Lenin's book. Whatever her minor flaws (to be discussed momentarily), she was absolutely right about the permanence of primitive accumulation – what much of imperialism and the contemporary world is about – in capitalism. Primitive accumulation means accumulation that violates the capitalist 'law of value', i.e. non-exchange of equivalents, beginning with the emptying of the English countryside in early modern history (16th to 19th centuries) by what would today be called 'economic reforms'.[1]

Much of the Marxist 'economics' (an oxymoron for the Marxist critique of political economy, an undertaking having a different 'object of study' than any 'economics') of the 1970s and even some authors today focus on the mathematical formulas in the first part of vol. III of *Capital* to adequately describe the root cause of capitalist crisis. And as important as these chapters on the rate of profit are, they make the big assumption that the concrete processes of social reproduction to which they refer are in fact being reproduced. (Social reproduction, in a nutshell, means replacing if not expanding used up machinery, materials and infrastructure, on one hand, and permitting today's working population to raise a future generation of people capable of working with contemporary technology on the other.)

Luxemburg, in her *Anti-Kritik* rebuttal to critics of her 1913 masterpiece (and on this I follow her 100 percent) argued that the issue here is not a matter of mathematics, but one of concrete analysis of real processes. When Western capital sucks Third World labour power, whose costs of reproduction it did not pay for, into the world division of labour, whether in Indonesia or in Los Angeles, that's primitive accumulation. When capital loots the natural environment and does not pay the replacement costs for that damage, that's primitive accumulation. When capital runs capital plant and infrastructure into the ground (the story of much of the US and the UK economies since the 1960s) that's primitive accumulation. When capital pays workers non-reproductive wages, (wages too low to produce a new generation of workers) that's primitive accumulation too. Lenin never discussed these things (if I recall, he rarely mentioned social reproduction) but Rosa Luxemburg wrote a whole book about it. To critics who want to dismiss these 'old' ideas with a complacent wave of the hand, I can only say that it's their loss.[2]

The problem is that the contemporary international left has inherited from the years just before and after World War I a theoretical framework, which is now mainly a highly problematic 'mood', in which Lenin's wrong-headed view, vulgarised by decades of further distortions by Stalinism, Maoism, Third Worldism and now by 'alterglobalism', has largely if not totally eclipsed Luxemburg's, particularly in its portrayal of the working class of the advanced capitalist sector (to my mind still the main force capable of positively superseding capitalism) as a quantité négligeable among the international forces for positive change.

Lenin's theory of imperialism and its bastard offspring reached the peak of their influence in the 1960s and '70s, when various national liberation struggles (Algeria, Indochina, Angola, Mozambique) and the Cuban Revolution constituted a 'tricontinental' constellation that seemed to be fulfilling the prediction that 'socialism' was the only way forward for the

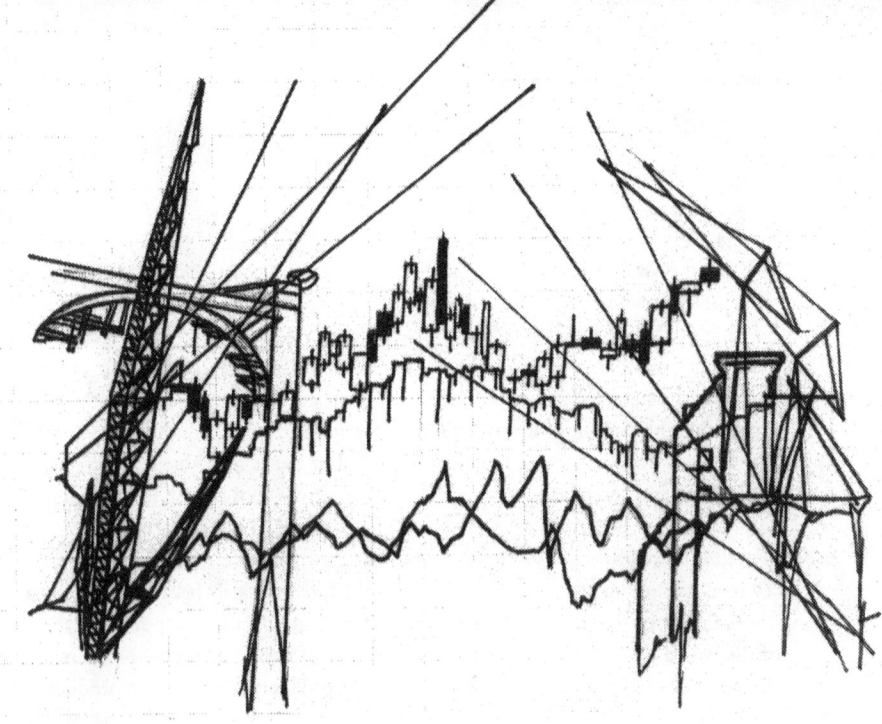

underdeveloped world. This ferment had taken off from the 1955 Bandung (Indonesia) conference of the 'non-aligned' (non-aligned in the Cold War) nations, with the cachet of such early anti-colonial figures as Nkrumah (Ghana), Sukarno (Indonesia), Nehru (India), and Nasser (Egypt). Unfortunately, the bureaucratic development regimes that triumphed in the 'tricontinental' countries were not socialist, and the western working class, which could have removed the weight of imperialism from their path, was absent at the rendez-vous. The Third Worldist 'tricontinental' world view was in shambles circa 1978-79 when Cambodia, Vietnam, China and the Soviet Union which had all at various times claimed the 'anti-imperialist' mantle, came close to going to war... with each other. What followed hard on this debacle was the past three decades' triumph of the neoliberal

'Washington consensus' in which the state centred development based on the old model was proclaimed unviable. During the high tide of the 'Washington consensus' the world has witnessed both an assault on the working class everywhere as well as on the old 'anti-imperialist' bloc, seriously reshaping both.

During this post-1977 period, the old lines of division between the 'advanced' and 'developing' world have blurred considerably. In the years of the 'Washington consensus' China and more recently Vietnam (from a very low base) have grown at rates unprecedented in the history of capitalism; India (from a similarly low base) has recently embarked on a similar path; 'new industrial countries' such as Korea and Taiwan have appeared; 'flying geese' countries such as Malaysia and Thailand, perhaps now Bangladesh (lowest wage country in the world, but now a textile power) have been pulled into the Asian boom; the Soviet bloc has collapsed and the European Union has absorbed most of its former Eastern European colonies; international labour migration to the West from Africa and Latin America has reached unprecedented levels, and Middle Eastern oil producers have been investing more of their revenues in regional development.

But most importantly, the bedrock of the world economy has shifted from the post-1945 North Atlantic connection between the US and Europe to the Pacific connection between US 'consumers' and Asia's producers, and above all China's. China's boom has in turn, through a frenetic demand for oil and raw materials, set off commodity booms in Latin America and parts of Africa.

At the same time, first the American and more recently the European working classes, which from 1965 to 1977 carried out the most sustained period of wildcat strikes in history, have been rolled back by a relentless combination of de-industrialisation, outsourcing and high-tech induced unemployment.

And while most of the past 30 years appear in capitalist terms to have been a 'boom' period, they have in fact been years of a steadily spreading precariousness for workers, peasants and marginal populations everywhere (even booming China has lost 20 million industrial jobs in the past

decade). Accompanying the glitz of new 'creative classes' from California to London to Warsaw to Shanghai and Mumbai, a huge upward shift of wealth has occurred. And the key to the whole period is, once again, fictitious capital.

Let us see how this is the case. I have invoked the good name of Rosa Luxemburg as the theoretical framework closest to my interpretation of Marx primarily because of her focus, inside and outside the pure capitalist system (cf. below) on the problematic of reproduction and non-reproduction. But, as indicated earlier, my framework differs somewhat from hers, and clarification imposes itself here. As will be seen, her framework has everything to do with the phenomena of imperialism and 'anti-imperialism' in the post-World War II era.

IMPURE CAPITALISM

Let's review what I consider some basics, which are not always self-evident. In this way we can go from contemporary history to abstract theory and back, and see the present in a new way. But to do so requires an examination of some basic ideas of Karl Marx.

Vol. I and most of vol. II of Marx's *Capital* are a phenomenology of a closed capitalist system in which there are only capitalists and wage labourers, and most of the focus is on the single firm. When, in the last section of vol. II, Marx shifts to the 'total social

the left has inherited Lenin's view of imperialism, further distorted by Stalinism, Maoism, Third Worldism and now 'alterglobalism'

capital' and expanded reproduction, he is moving beyond that heuristic model.[3]

That demarcation of the interaction of the 'pure system' (capitalists and wage labourers) with, on one hand, the vast modern population of unproductive consumers who live off surplus value and do not produce it, i.e. the FIRE (Finance-Insurance-Real Estate) sector, state civil servants, managerial strata, the military sector, the law enforcement/prison sector, and, on the other hand, with nature and with petty producers (today found primarily in the Third World), is fundamental for clarity. These strata in the advanced sector are dominated today by the same 'creative classes' mentioned above. None of the latter populations are present in vols. I and II of Marx's *Capital*, except for some interesting asides and the important chapters in the middle of vol. II dealing with insurance, bookkeeping and other 'faux frais' (false costs) of production (the latter having today burgeoned beyond belief relative to Marx's time). Capital is a circuit, (in vols. I and II), with simple reproduction, (i.e. an abstract assumption of 'zero growth') and is a spiral in expanded reproduction. A

commodity, whether from Dept. I (what Marx designated as the production of machines) or II (consumer goods) which does not complete the circuit, i.e. is not productively consumed in Dept. I (new means of production) or Dept. II (new labour power) ceases to be capital.[4] These definitions, which have been laughed out of the mainstream theories of 'economics' and which get surprisingly little attention even from some self-styled Marxists, allow us to reconceptualise the contemporary world economy and make clear distinctions between real wealth and costs that are merely costs of maintaining the status quo.[5]

Rosa Luxemburg also had the great merit of emphasising capitalism as a transitional mode of production between European feudalism and socialism. This may seem a truism, but it is much more than that. In her survey of the rise and fall of classical political economy from the Physiocrats to the Ricardian school, she points out that only a socialist (i.e. Marx) could solve the problem of the source of profit and of expanded reproduction. To wit: capitalism must be seen as a necessarily incomplete, transient mode of production, which lives in part off the pre-capitalist modes it looted and continues to loot, and whose full crisis is only visible to someone seeing 'beyond' it to a higher mode. Capitalism is therefore a system in which no practical viewpoint, either of an individual capitalist or of the total social capital, or finally of labour power as a commodity (the class-in-itself) can be 'concretely universal', that is capable of practically acting on real problems. All viewpoints on capital 'within' the system, including 'class-in-itself' struggles of individual groups of workers, are 'negation of the negation' viewpoints, and only the perspective that looks prior to and beyond capitalism can be a 'self-subsisting positive' with a universal (class for itself) programme. From the Italian pirates of the 11th century to the slave labour in the Dominican Republic or Brazil today, capitalism has never stopped its 'looting' of labour power and resources 'outside' the closed (vols. I and II) system of exchange of equivalents. Thus the ongoing presence of capital's initial looting of non-capitalist sources of wealth, for Luxemburg, also points to the possibility of its barbaric end (of which interwar fascism was more than a foretaste), if it is not positively superseded by proletarian revolution.

Next, and this is fundamental, capital does not appear to capitalists as 'self-expanding value' or a 'social relationship of production' (bedrock

terms of Marx having no practical meaning or even existing from the 'negation of the negation' viewpoints of central bankers, hedge fund managers or trade union bureaucrats within the system); it appears to them as titles to wealth, namely to profit, interest and ground rent, whose value is determined over the course of a business cycle not by the fine points of the opening chapters of *Capital* vol. III but as a capitalisation of anticipated future cash flow. Marx, of course, only introduces such titles to wealth – stocks, bonds, leases – after first presenting the heuristic pure system, setting it in motion in the final chapters of *Capital* vol. II (expanded reproduction), and then discussing the determination of price and the rate of profit in the opening sections of *Capital* vol. III. Capital as capitalists know it, up to and including all the new 'financial products' of the past 25 years such as derivatives and hedge funds, are 'liens' on the total cash flow representing, ultimately, the total surplus value produced in the 'pure system' AND supplemented by LOOT (non-reproductive exchange) outside and eventually inside the system. We know very well that over long periods of a capitalist cycle these 'liens' can depart widely from the price/value determinations that ultimately regulate the cash flow on which they draw, until they are deflated in the periodic crash.

But the source of that total profit/total surplus value is an empirical question, not to be settled by abstract resort to different takes on the 'transformation of value into prices' (an important but overplayed debate among Marxist academics) or possible flaws in the reproduction schema of *Capital* vol. II. Are capital plant (means of production, infrastructure) and labour power being reproduced or not? Does the 'consumption' of an electronic battlefield or a new prison or a yacht expand or contract social reproduction? Such a question immediately takes us from the realm of pure theory (however fundamental) to the concrete historical operation of the system.

The relationship between the value of the myriad capitalist titles to wealth and the surplus value and loot on which they draw is, of course, not an arbitrary one.

Let's go back to the pure system, only capitalists and workers, no banks, no other distorting 'titles to wealth'. Let us further imagine that the entire world is capitalist and that everything exchanges at its value. In such a world, with rising productivity over time, a greater and greater mass of capital is set in motion by a smaller total amount of living labour, the exploitation of the latter being (for Marx) the source of all profit. Hence (with many ups and downs along the way) the rate of profit capable of sustaining all those titles, unless adequately supplemented by what I have called 'loot', declines historically.

But, as Luxemburg points out in her *Anti-Kritik*, the falling rate of profit does not prompt the capitalists to 'hand the factory keys over to the working class'. Her framework enabled her to see how capitalism could ultimately destroy society – barbarism, in her words, or the 'mutual destruction of the contending classes' as the *Communist Manifesto* put it in 1847 – by being required to turn more and more to primitive accumulation and non-reproduction, a prophecy we see materialising before our eyes today.

Capital, for Marx, (and here we open up a dimension not discussed by Luxemburg) through the pursuit of profit by a myriad of individual capitalists, ultimately destroys itself, becomes a barrier to itself, by pushing the productive forces to a point where the socially necessary time of reproduction, based on the reproductive value of labour power, can no longer serve as the 'numeraire', the common denominator, for the daily functioning of the system. Capital requires living

Loren Goldner

labour to exist, and for labour power's value to be the numeraire, and it simultaneously, through innovation, expels living labour from the production process and undermines the numeraire. That is the pure model's fundamental contradiction.

Of course, the pure model of capitalism has never existed and never will exist. As we know, titles to wealth (profit, interest, ground rent), central banks regulating the markets of such titles, and a state enforcing such titles all pre-existed the full blown triumph of capitalism, i.e. the transformation of means of production and labour power into commodities as the dominant source of wealth.

Once we add titles to wealth to the pure model, as Marx does in the middle and concluding sections of vol. III of *Capital*, we see a different picture. It is precisely because of these titles and because of capitalism's ability to loot non-capitalist populations and nature that we do NOT, over long cycles, see any mechanical fall in the capitalist rate of profit. Such titles tend to correspond to the underlying value, or fall below it, mainly at the end of one cycle (through deflation) and the beginning of the next one. The deflationary crisis acts as a form of 'retroactive planning' that re-equilibrates the capitalists' titles to wealth with the underlying rate of profit generated within the pure system. This was obvious in the 19th century, when such a crisis occurred every ten years or so (1808 – 1819 – 1827 – 1837

– 1846 – 1857 – 1866 – 1873, etc.) It is less obvious in the period since 1914 when the state has much more actively attempted to preserve capitalist valuations against devalorisation by techniques usually associated with 'Keynesianism'. We are of course, in 2007, in the midst of probably the biggest fictitious credit bubble in the history of capitalism. What we have been living through, particularly since the early 1970s, has been a huge operation of credit pyramiding, managed by the world's central banks, aimed at PRESERVING the paper value of existing titles to wealth, and a significant transfer of working class wages and capital not invested in either plant or infrastructure to help prop up those titles. That latter phenomenon is what I call the 'self-cannibalisation' of the system when the 'primitive accumulation' mechanism turns inward, i.e. non-reproduction, as referred to above.

Luxemburg of course did not live to see either the post-1933 American or German versions of quasi-permanent military production, supported by the taxation of the working class, and still less the post-1944 Bretton Woods system, in which the US financial markets and the US State acquired the ability to tap wealth from every part of the capitalist world (until recently, minus Russia and China) through dollar seigniorage (the latter referring to the 'free lunch' acquired through the US's 'maintaining empire through

US imperialism has perfected the strategy of 'managing empire through bankruptcy'

bankruptcy').[6] And quite obviously, credit has increased a thousand times in significance since Luxemburg's time, as a way of temporarily prolonging business cycles, while changing nothing of the fundamental contradictions in play.

The implicit final stage of this process is, once again, the self-cannibalisation of the system, if and when the sources of loot outside the 'closed system' are exhausted. We have not yet seen this in dramatic form in the case of the era of US world hegemony. But history does provide the example of the Nazi period in Germany, when Hjalmar Schacht, Hitler's finance minister, ran up a huge debt pyramid to finance German rearmament in the 1933-1938 period, while holding real wages at 50 percent of 1929 levels. The difference between Germany then and the US today is that Germany had been shorn of most of its external sources of loot after its defeat in 1918, and hence had to seize some new ones militarily after 1938.

Something similar could happen in the US-centred system if and when the US loses its ability to tap wealth throughout the world with dollar denominated accumulation, and one can, without exaggeration, see US foreign policy today as a worldwide extension of the underlying dynamic of German expansion under Hitler, minus the total internal implosion of American society – so far.

Thus I would 'correct' Luxemburg to the extent that the external relations of the 'pure system' are not so much about the sale of a surplus product on the model of the sale of industrial goods to independent farmers or peasants (though that of course also takes place) as the more important circulation of an ever increasing fictitious bubble (fictitious capital) through international loans in exchange for whatever loot can be acquired from petty producers' labour power or from nature. I argue that this fictitious bubble is initially lawfully generated WITHIN the pure system and is discussed in Marx's middle chapters of *Capital* vol. III. This is the NECESSARY, internally generated reason that the system requires permanent primitive accumulation.

Let's see why this is the case. Back to the closed system, to which we have added capitalist titles to wealth, capitalisations of an anticipated cash

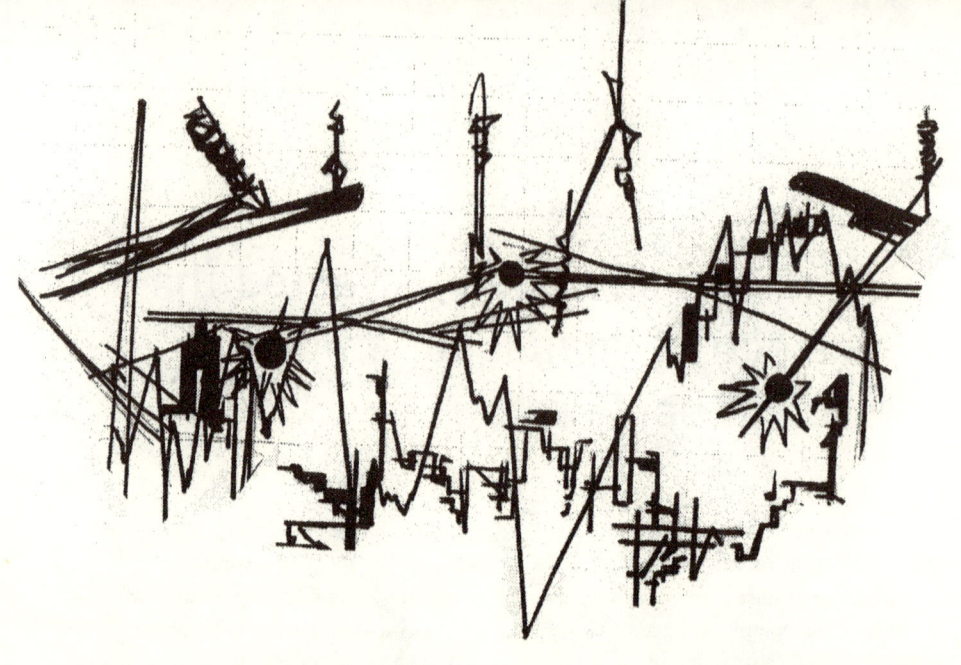

flow. These titles of course go together with a capital market, a central bank and a state enforcing them, and ultimately a state debt (again, all *Capital* vol. III phenomena).

Because capitalism is an anarchic system, (a 'heteronomic' system in Kant's sense) a practical perspective on the total social capital which could keep these capitalisations (most immediately, stocks) rigorously in line with the underlying (current reproductive cost) value of the assets on whose cash flow they depend is a chimera. Increases in labour productivity, particularly those which ripple quickly through the whole system, such as canal and railroad construction in the 19th century, or the air, shipping and communications innovations of recent decades, are not immediately registered in the capitalised value of all assets. Over time, such innovations create, rather, a fictitious increment 'f' of overvalued capitalisations (titles to cash flow)

which must be periodically purged in a deflationary collapse, as we saw in the dotcom frenzy of the 1990's and the dotcom crash of 2000. The actions of the central bank in regulating credit markets aim at preserving at least some of the capitalised titles to wealth from the devalorisation (deflation) demanded by increased labour productivity. The credit markets, the central bank and the state debt are all designed to 'manage' the increasing disparity between total titles to wealth – the fictitious bubble – and their pure system value as long as possible, though official ideology would rarely if ever state the problem so baldly.

I would argue, therefore, that this internally generated, 'pure system' ball of hot air, FICTITIOUS CAPITAL (fictitious relative to the real current reproductive value of assets) is, more than real goods, what is 'exported' in exchange for loot. As long as sufficient loot compensates for the fictitious gap, accumulation can continue. This is my (minor) disagreement with Luxemburg.

The fictitious bubble in the contemporary world is first of all the huge ($3-4 trillion, at current, conservative estimates) dollar 'overhang', the net US external debt ($11-12 trillion held abroad, minus $8 imperialism', in which a diffuse 'Porto Alegre'/World Social Forum mood today enlists such 'progressive' forces as Hugo Chavez, Hezbollah, Hamas, the Iranian mullahs, the Taliban, the Iraqi 'resistance', and perhaps tomorrow Kim Jong-il;

How much longer will China, Korea, the Middle East, Japan and Russia hold a declining dollar?

trillion in US assets overseas), held mainly in central banks. Everything, from a capitalist viewpoint, must be done to prevent its deflation. The US government is busy depreciating it by its 'managing empire through bankruptcy', and its foreign creditors fret at the erosion of their holdings. But they re-lend the money to the US government and US financial markets, making possible more domestic US credit, more consumption, and more imports from America's creditors, because for now the collapse of the dollar would be their collapse as well, and they as yet see no alternative.

If the preceding is correct, it constitutes an alternative view of imperialism to that of Lenin (still upheld today by myriad Trotskyists, for starters). The political issue for the left as I see it is not so much imperialism, which I take as a given, but the ideology of 'anti-

yesterday it included Saddam Hussein. Post-1945 and particularly post-1973 developments have been blurring the lines on the old 'anti-imperialist' road map.

We see US world hegemony disintegrating faster than we generally imagined possible (almost recalling the speed of the collapse of the Soviet bloc). Out of this disintegration, what will emerge? Proletarian revolution? I hope so. But what could also emerge, as the US emerged in 1945 on the ruins of the British empire, is a new centre of world accumulation, most likely, as indicated, centred in Asia.

Suppose, in some yet to be concretised scenario, China and Japan (who, despite the rhetoric, have ever closer economic ties), along with the tigers (e.g. Korea, Taiwan) and the 'flying geese' (Malaysia, Thailand, etc.) manage to constitute an economic bloc, an Asian currency. Given geopolitical realities, and above all US opposition (as evidenced during the 1997-98 Asia crisis, when it nixed the creation of an Asian Monetary Fund proposed by Japan), it's hard to imagine this happening without some equivalent of World War II in whose outcome the US, Russia and India will all have a stake. If this reorganisation became the basis of a new phase of capitalist expansion, comparable to the US centred expansion of 1945-1975, would it somehow be any more 'progressive' than the US dominated phase?

The question, then, along the way, is how to situate the various world forces in play as the US declines.

Chavez, the latest 'anti-imperialist' hero, recently made a world tour that included such... progressive... states as Belarus, Russia, Iran and China. Latin America is booming right now because of exports to China. Parts of Africa, again, are reviving for the same reason. This currently comes back to the 'indebted US consumer', and a collapse of the dollar empire would stop the music – for a while. But as a Japanese minister, weary of the growing dollar reserves in the Bank of Japan, said not too long ago: 'give us 15 years, and we won't need the US'. With the dollar declining by the day on world exchanges, how much longer will the Chinese, the Koreans, the Japanese, the Middle Eastern oil sheiks, the Russians, the Venezuelans, and the Medillin drug cartel – all major holders of dollars – be willing to hold onto a depreciating asset? And if out of this debacle a new pole of capitalist accumulation does emerge, whether or not it includes 'old' imperialist powers (e.g. Japan and Russia), will it be 'progressive'?

That, to me, is THE question which the theoreticians still working off the Leninist model of 'anti-imperialism' have to answer. How much longer can the international left be offering 'critical support' or 'military support' to the Taliban before it finds itself, as so many times in the past, the ideological midwife of a new reactionary constellation?

FOOTNOTES

1

The 'law of value' was part of Marx's qualitative break with the classical political economy of Smith and Ricardo. All three emphasised the centrality of the social time required to produce a commodity, though Marx's understanding was also quite different. All agreed in rejecting swindle and arbitrary price markups as an explanation of profit, but against Smith and Ricardo's inability to explain capitalist profit otherwise, Marx demonstrated that it came from the time the worker had to work each day in excess of the value of his or her labour power (i.e. of the time necessary for simply reproducing the worker as worker). Later theories of 'monopoly capitalism', most famously Lenin's, also threw the law of value and socially necessary labour time out the window as a phenomenon of Marx's time which capitalism had transcended in their own, in its supposed 'monopoly phase', in which cartels supposedly controlled prices and collected 'super-profits'.

2

Some people on other occasions have objected to my use of the term 'primitive accumulation' for contemporary capitalism, insisting that for Marx the term meant only the initial separation of producers from the means of production. I would just like to say that if 'primitive accumulation' is too specifically linked to that initial separation in the 16th-17th century, then we have to develop another term to describe the forms of capitalist loot (in contrast to profit generated by 'normal' exploitation). In addition to Luxemburg, I also take the term from its usage by the Soviet left opposition theorist Preobrazhensky (in *The New Economics*) and his argument for 'socialist primitive accumulation' in the 1920s: organising a managed decline of the Russian peasantry through selling industrial goods dear and buying agricultural goods cheap. (Let's not get distracted by the unhappy outcome of that strategy).

I'll say again that when capital interacts with nature and petty producers outside the wage-labour relationship, and when it pushes wages and capital expenditure below reproductive costs inside that relationship, it is violating the 'exchange of equivalents' which Marx saw as the 'heuristic' framework for separating capitalist profits and accumulation from swindle, monopoly, selling goods above their value, and other wrong headed explanations of profit. And if we don't want to call that non-reproduction 'primitive accumulation', fine, but let's first admit that such phenomena exist, and (since the 1970s) are increasingly important, and moreover indispensable to the system.

3

'Expanded reproduction' refers to normal capitalist accumulation, in which a part of the annual surplus is reinvested in new equipment and new labour power, in contrast to the heuristic 'simple reproduction' assumed for most of vols. I and II, in which such expansion is artificially bracketed.

4

OK, a tank, a guided missile, a McMansion or a Ferrari belong in neither department, but are consumption of the capitalist class.

5

Marx in *Capital* vol. III introduces those factions of the capitalist class which derive their income from the financial markets and from rents, but the masses of people today who are outside the 'pure system' in the capitalist heartland, such as FIRE-sector employees, state civil servants or corporate managerial strata, are for the most part implicit in all of *Capital*. That hardly means that, with their huge unproductive consumption today, they are any less important.

6

If the US, for example, compels China to revalue its currency by 10 percent, 10 percent of the Chinese goods its dollar holdings represent become free tribute to the US.

Loren Goldner is a writer and activist based in New York City. His latest book Herman Melville (2006) is available through Amazon. Most of his work is available on the Break Their Haughty Power website:
http://home.earthlink.net/~lrgoldner

WAITING FOR THE END OF THE WORLD

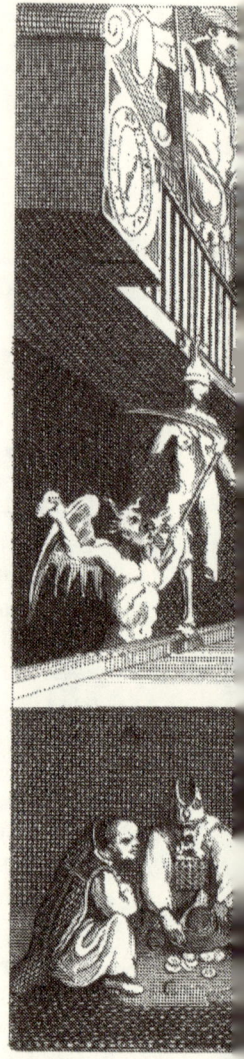

Would a financial crisis mean recession, depression or revolution? And haven't we been waiting a long time for this liberating, or devastating, catastrophe? <u>Jeff Strahl</u> surveys the prophets and naysayers and gives his own take on 'a global crisis of unprecedented proportions'

E xpectation of a global economic collapse is a lot like waiting for Godot. It even features a 'first coming', namely the 1929 crash and subsequent global depression. Such a development has been described innumerable times in the last century. But the discussion has become very lively in the last few months, due to factors such as the crisis in the sub-prime housing loans market, increasing attention to ballooning debt levels of all sorts, and rising global trade tensions.

Mainstream media discussion has of course largely discounted the very possibility of a global economic collapse ever since... the last collapse. The argument usually revolved around the assertion that regulatory measures adopted during and after the 1930s make such a collapse pretty impossible, including the preclusion of disastrous trade conflicts due to the world economic structure becoming more and more integrated, and the stakes all national capitals have in

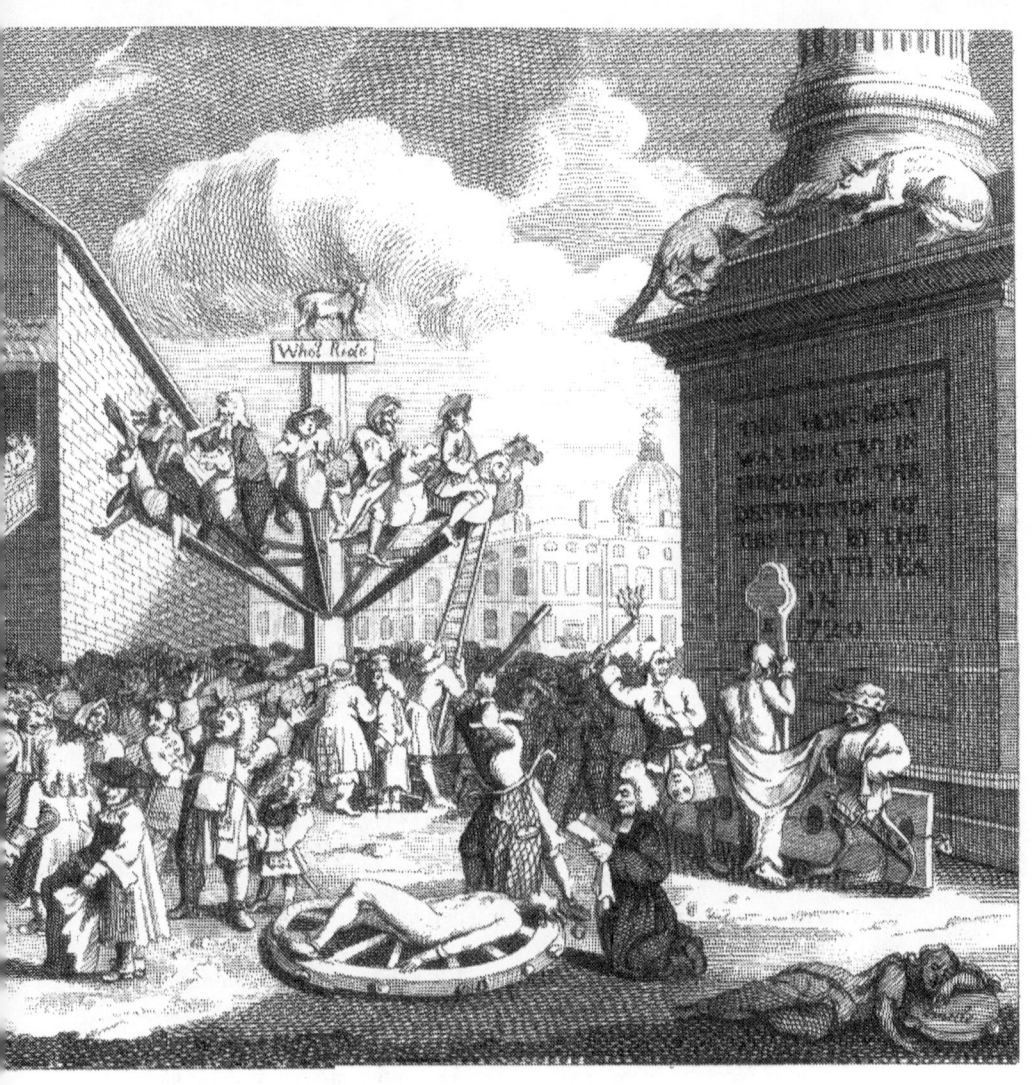

Image: William Hogarth,
Emblematical Print of the South Sea
Bubble, 1721 (reprinted 1809)

Living in a Bubble

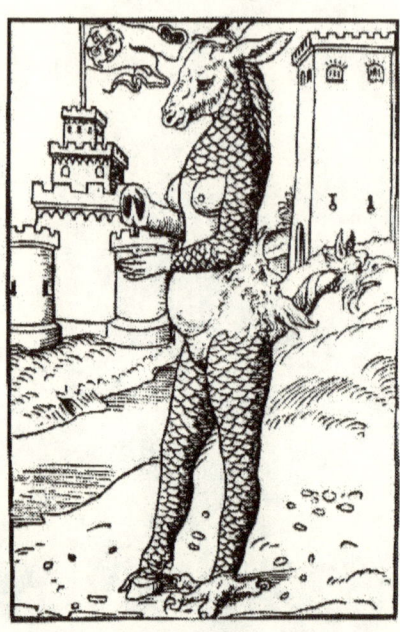

making sure that cooperation continues. This consensus even includes much of what passes for left media, e.g., *Left Business Observer*, whose editor Doug Henwood is regularly called upon to provide commentary on 'progressive' media outlets such as Pacifica Radio, during which he downplays any possibility of a catastrophic crisis.[1] Henwood and his cohorts have of course generally come to adopt neo-Keynesian perspectives, even when they still claim an affinity with Marxist analysis, describe problems as basically the results of corporate greed and incompetent right-wing policy makers, and prescribe little more than traditional liberal palliatives such as a hike in the minimum wage and higher taxes on the rich.

Outside this consensus, one sees analysts such as James Petras, who pens articles on the state of global capital such as 'Crisis of US Capitalism or the Crisis of the US Wage and Salaried Worker?'[2] He contends that, from the perspective of capital, everything is just fine. Mega-corporations are making money, there is no profitability crisis, no crisis of capital whatsoever, and exploitation is going on as normal.

Further along, we have people with occasionally vaguely left politics who do see a mounting problem with the global economy in particular due to the debt situation, who predict that a major crisis is looming, but eschew the notion that such a crisis would afflict the capitalist system as a whole. Rather it would be confined to the US, or only affect the set up of the system as it is right now, i.e., under US control and domination. Mike Whitney has written a series of articles on the mounting liquidity crisis, including one in which he asserts that what's needed is a new

Image: Pope-ass, Medieval harbinger of the end of the world. Socialism or bestiary?

The possibility of a global collapse has been discounted ever since... the last collapse

compact of cooperation between labour and capital.[3] Henry Liu also sees the crisis as one which will primarily impact the US, leading to a new era of supremacy in the world market for what he calls China's 'market socialism'.[4] Former US Treasury Department official (in the Carter administration) Richard Cook espouses 'reforms' such as social credit, an idea discredited back in the 1930s (when it was popular with Fascists), but who remembers?[5]

Then we have those who see a generalised global collapse as becoming increasingly likely, and predict that its onset will pretty automatically produce a situation which will lead to a revolution. These include 'Anticipation Laboratory' Leap2020 and various ultra-left sects.[6] The idea is that mass degradation will push people to realise that the capitalist system itself is at fault, that it is unsustainable, and that human happiness, indeed our very survival, will require a total transformation of the system. This is held in spite of the failure of past episodes of mass crisis, including the '30s, to actually lead to such a turn of events.

The nature of the crisis is such that reformist measures, if ever they could work, no longer are able to do so. One needs to remember that Marx's analysis of capital was in its rawest, most fundamental form, based upon an admittedly fictitious (albeit valid in essential ways) situation of a single global capital facing the entire world's population of wage workers. Capital survives by forcing that population to work a full day while only a decreasing fraction of that day is equivalent to the socially necessary labour time required to produce what it takes for that population to survive as wage workers under the given conditions. All labour performed in addition to socially necessary labour time (i.e. the time it takes for the worker to produce enough to meet her own needs) is surplus value, the source of all profits. Hence, surplus value is produced under a global process, while the actually-existing individual capitals (i.e. companies and businesses) appropriate shares of this surplus via market interactions which have less and less to do with the actual portions of the surplus that they produce, if indeed they produce any.

Jeff Strahl

global economic collapse will be more like sinking into a patch of quicksand than going over a cliff

All crises of capital, including the fundamental one of the tendency of the rate of profit to fall, are rooted in this dynamic, whose tendency is the expulsion of living labour, the only source of surplus value.[7]

However, this is generally not visible if one were to look at market data, as market interactions are reflective only of prices. Prices of commodities are at best only an approximation of their values, the socially necessary labour time expended in their production. Increasingly, prices diverge from values, especially as more and more activity takes place in the realm of circulation, as opposed to production. And financial speculation increases the abstraction from values ever more. In an era of derivatives, bets are made not on industries but on instruments of... financial speculation, e.g. stocks. Reckoning comes only when the imbalances become totally unsupportable, much as a structure made up of cards may become unstable long before that last card causes it to collapse. But global economic collapse is far more likely to be experienced as sinking into a patch of quicksand than as going over a cliff.

Mechanisms set up after WWII with the intention of regulating domestic economic systems as well as the world market are unable to deal with capital's fundamental contradiction, not even remotely acknowledged by mainstream economists, or even many 'left' ones. All they have managed to do is push the contradictions to the side, to defer the crisis, at the cost of making the contradictions ever deeper, as for example in building a debt bubble that is far in excess of anything else ever experienced. Increasingly, counter-measures being undertaken only make matters worse, or ameliorate one symptom by making others even more accentuated.

Furthermore, this is coming on top of a crisis in the real physical world which serves as a setting for capitalist production. This comes in the form of degradation of the environment, e.g. global warming, contamination by toxic chemicals of land, air and sea, species die-offs. And it comes in the form of resource depletion, be it of the soil, or supplies of raw materials vital for production -- most importantly that of oil and natural gas, which provide the cheap energy that has made the global production system viable in the first place.

A global crisis of unprecedented proportions is thus increasingly likely, I'd say impossible to avoid. But people committed to a fundamental transformation of society cannot simply sit back and let it happen and hope all turns out alright. Given the past, there is a good chance (in fact, it is more likely) that those whose material conditions are driven way down by developments will turn to some charismatic figure who promises deliverance by some sort of reformist programme, or by waging war to secure resources for 'our nation', or a combination of the two.

This is, of course, not the '30s. On one hand, people are now even less connected to the land than they were then, more detached from any sort of culture which consists of something beyond the consumption of goods and images, and more cynical about the possibility of radical social change; 'the 1960s' or the Soviet experience supposedly show that striving for this brings chaos or something worse than what one started with. On the other hand there is less room for any Keynesian or other reformist measures to provide even temporary relief.

Why not? Massive state spending is not a viable option when debts are already maxed out. And a resort to global war, which is what ultimately ended the 1930s depression, is problematic in an era in which such warfare could easily result in the extinction of human life, or at the very least its descent into barbarism. When it really comes down to it, it's up to us as a species as to how we get out of this alive, and we have no time to lose, the hour's getting late.

FOOTNOTES

1

http://www.leftbusinessobserver.com

2

http://www.globalresearch.ca/index.php?context=va&aid=2763

3

http://www.dissidentvoice.org/2007/05/swan-song-for-the-democrats/

4

http://www.atimes.com/atimes/China_Business/IE23Cb03.html

5

http://www.globalresearch.ca/index.php?context=va&aid=5905

6

http://www.leap2020.eu

7

Living labour is Marx's term for human labour that creates both new use values and new exchange value. Living labour valorises – that is, increases the value of – invested capital.

Jeff Strahl is a long-time San Francisco Bay Area activist

RISKY BUSINESS

With the prospect of earning over the odds on derivatives trading, hedge fund managers are employing ever more high-tech means to calculate risk and predict stock market activity. But Wall Street's faith in its own predictive powers often blinds investors to the fundamental laws of investment, says risk specialist <u>Stanley Morgan</u>

A friend of mine was working as a quant at a Wall Street investment bank when a large and well-known hedge fund, Long Term Capital Management, went bust in 1998. Experts from a number of top financial firms were called in to help stanch the bleeding and prevent the disaster from spreading to the larger financial system. My friend was one of the people enlisted to sift through the mess and figure out exactly where the fund stood. Afterward, when I asked him how things looked, he shook his head in amazement: the people he'd spoken with at the fund had no clue about half of what they owned or what it was worth. Granted, complex derivative securities (the kind this fund had been miserably unsuccessful gambling with) can be exceedingly hard to price even when you're not in the midst of financial turmoil, but that's something you need to take into account when you're managing billions of dollars of other people's money. The fact that this fund lost enough in a week to nearly bring down the economy was a sign that its managers were playing Russian roulette with bazookas, not simply 'investing'.

This kind of financial brinkmanship is becoming increasingly popular. Warren Buffett has called derivatives – which often encapsulate extremely complex relationships between multiple products or events, and allow you to take on risk many times greater than the actual money you have invested – 'financial weapons of mass destruction'. Derivatives are over-used and routinely mispriced such that companies are often giving an inaccurate accounting of the value of their holdings. And when things don't work out the way you expect, derivatives can cause staggering losses. There will be more and bigger blowups. You don't have to be Chicken Little to acknowledge that large pieces of the sky are falling all the time – from Barings Bank ('95) to hedge funds Long Term Capital Management ('98), Julian Robertson's Tiger Fund ('02) and Amaranth ('06). The particular excuse is almost irrelevant: 'That surprise move in Brazilian interest rates was a 1 in 1,000,000,000,000,000 occurrence'; 'The liquidity in that Russian mining stock suddenly dried up, so I couldn't unwind my position' – sure, but that's not going to bring your money back (or mine, if I was unlucky enough to be one of your investors). Trading desks are increasingly speculating in products they don't fully understand, using computer models that don't account for that deadly one-in-a-trillion possibility (what author/trader Nassim Nicholas Taleb calls a 'black swan'), and at the same time generally shunning anything that appears too simple and comprehensible. Why?

One culprit is a familiar one on Wall Street: greed. If you think Dell will go from $25 to $75, you can buy a thousand shares and make $50 thousand, or you can buy some call options and make many times that amount with the same investment. Or you can use borrowed money to increase your leverage even more. Yeah, but what if Dell ends up *dropping* to $15? Hedge funds have brought the use of leverage to a point never dreamed of before, while hedging the resulting risk in ways that are not necessarily foolproof. But precisely because of the massive leverage they use, hedge funds hold out the promise of returns that dwarf the boring S&P 500 or FTSE. And they often deliver them – until that statistically impossible move in Brazilian interest rates happens. Like the entrepreneurs who sold shovels during the California gold rush, the smart money knows that the best way to get rich from a hedge fund is by *running* one. Fund managers take their cut off the top: they get 2 percent of your money no matter what their performance. The fund's other investors take their chances, and feel most of the pain if the fund's bets don't pan out. Still, people who can afford the price of admission are drawn to hedge funds' potential returns, their exclusivity, and their general sexiness like moths to a flame, adding billions of hopeful dollars a week to the pool. The result: more

Stanley Morgan

traders increasingly use computer models to speculate in products they don't understand, shunning simple and comprehensible investments

pressure to pump up returns, more leverage, more borrowing, more complex derivatives, more precarious and hard-to-quantify dependencies between products and trading desks. And more risk.

A less obvious reason for the explosion in the use of leverage, and the concomitant increase in 'systemic risk', is 21st century Wall Street's love of technological solutions almost for their own sake. Sure, it costs a lot of money to hire an army of physics PhDs and build computer models that can run through a million scenarios a second, but who wants to be seen scratching out calculations on a yellow legal pad? If you're marketing yourself as a financial genius – or if you 'are' one, like the Nobel Prize winners who founded Long Term Capital – you'd better have a flashier plan to show your investors than 'these three stocks look really cheap'. But while strategists crank out incomprehensible new products and Rube Goldberg-esque mechanisms for managing their inherent risk (usually imperfectly), there is plenty of money

being made using the mundane strategy of looking for mispriced securities – 'Buy low, sell high' – with no chance of losing three thousand times your initial investment.

The annual 'rich lists' continue to be dominated by traditional businessmen (technology, steel, retail, media) who make money in ways that would be recognisable to a 19th century capitalist and old-style investors like Warren Buffett, who claims not to even have a quote machine in his office. For the most part, the rich continue to get richer in the traditional ways. As for the new hedge-fund billionaires, the financial rock stars of the moment (with earnings in the hundreds of millions of dollars a year), they make their money largely from fees paid to them by very rich people – not a very high-tech way to earn a living, but they don't seem to be complaining.

Stanley Morgan builds risk-management systems for a Wall Street investment bank

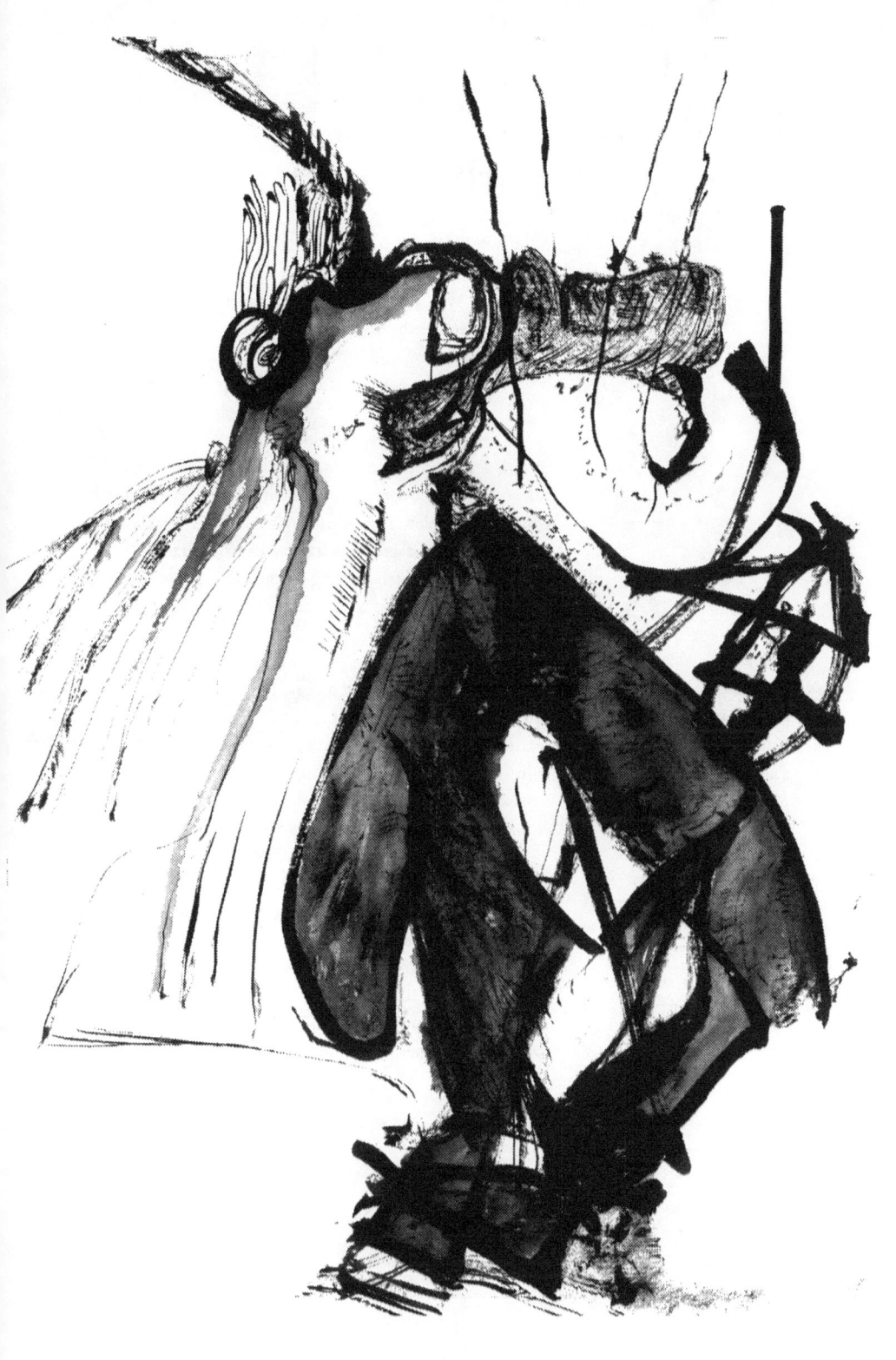

FALLING IN LOVE CREAM CRAB
by Keston Sutherland

Now itch like precision flamecutting. Detected sweat in
bloom Pakistani Sukhoi-30MKI,
sweat that eyes in the front of your head crunch,
pulse on detergent, broken ear on Anantnag
bus ride flowering to a throat full of sweat,
brighter than the consumption reel it cap fades for

no-one half

se

by half second and is nothing except love there
is nothing except it on. Back flowing fade
you point a skeleton at, sweat on it
on it is the wool/teeth foreclosures ½ off skeleton,
the no-one your flesh is slung on burning its
with desire FTIR spectr. In China the

©

Let Us Put You

touch into dead green: hit aflame by
lips switched cutting the dead air dead volts
scattered by holding your face on dying
palms in the thrill of a kiss you cry for—
a bat drops. Planets drop in. A bat
stopgap for the IAF. Make more by working

cry for—

less

life TBA by my shred hands wringing the bridge by
Dartford into • *clavicle sorbet*, • new *tibia bake*,
new *uln* / under you grabbing your face act
calm orgasming frantically in you needing you
would the person whose car is parked
to esteem the pram full of scissors in Morgan Stanley,

Houston,

Taipei,

Now expand into the Netherlands. Into the
line booster fade you point a skeleton at

---

it is the skeleton imagined dead; its mirroring in
your faced life not at a time forever not for
anything scratched in patty where the reverse is
true to mere form, dying. Get out
                                    bed
                                    of
• new *Lumbar Vertebrae Ranch Squid*, / nail—skip to •
Preparation Tips in Frum Mix, set shaking
unfree of its off switch, broken on the heart pro
rata cut while you wait. You make dinner with
Nancy Zucker Boswell from Transparency International
look stupid. You sheathe the IAF in ice,
                                    faster
                                    than
reason is your immediacy. Wait and see
it. It is nothing except love, its cast of paroxysms gets
the dead air plastered, abiding in Asset Liability
Management • new 1 John 3.17 ia bak McNamara
to Wolfowitz his brother in need and closes
negotiations on the master derivatives Sunny Delight
                                    Kids Cove
                                    lockout and riot
leatherette integument for the bat. It drops
are on hold. You have been placed in a queue
on hold. You have been placed in a queue are
Verkehr in the community, substitute to produce
alternative
puns with fakir, with quaere, and finally
with hair, i.e., hair in the community, in its throat sweat,
                                    free fish
                                    oil for kids

Now get nowhere fast. Anantnag running on
the pram full of hedging needs in Ann Veneman X

Living in a Bubble

paroxysmic you arise, just now sincerely
Chinese for the first time, locking your car.
The temperature is at 3480. We deliver.
Love is the angle of the mirroring it breaks for,
                              the pivot
                              are bet
you on track for. Nothing but love in the face that
aflame steel discolours red. You remember
kissing my mouth, traducing the oxyacetylene
whisper cut out. Later in the ear I
again am in an encounter with the skeleton you
point at going. There are feet everywhere
                              you tread
                              on
them cap with your 1.6 way mirror • new *tarsals*, • •
1. credit aspect 7, plastic 8 way meet clients'
hold you—throttle out sex in Palam debt product,
your eyes a must-see, icing as they flower in
beauty vanilla bonds • n. What this means is that
placed in a face they flash out incomparably
                              wild back
                              flowing fade
and I love you really there is nothing but love over
it is all there is there nothing other
than it no there by where the cylinders are fitted
patella bol with regulators and flexible hoses which lead
to the blowpipe. It will make your mouth water
freeze, a life aflame in the shark shit,
                              only now forever,
                              1.9

Area Strategic Partnerships
AIM
communities this will include
tackling health inequalities and
including Culture and Leisure for all'

—notably for a socially irresponsible, easily credited, deeply indebted, multi-mortgaged suburban or 'boorjoy' class loafing in mentally undemanding Bluetooth-ed multi-tasking tick-a-box make-work.

Area Strategic Partnerships
OVERVIEW
relates to Crime and Disorder:
Strategy Managers are to explain
within a Low Crime Environment'

—while a subhuman semi-crazed underclass infests the decaying urban terraces, council 'sink estates', social housing association developments and home-owner settlements of urban, suburban and rural Middle England.

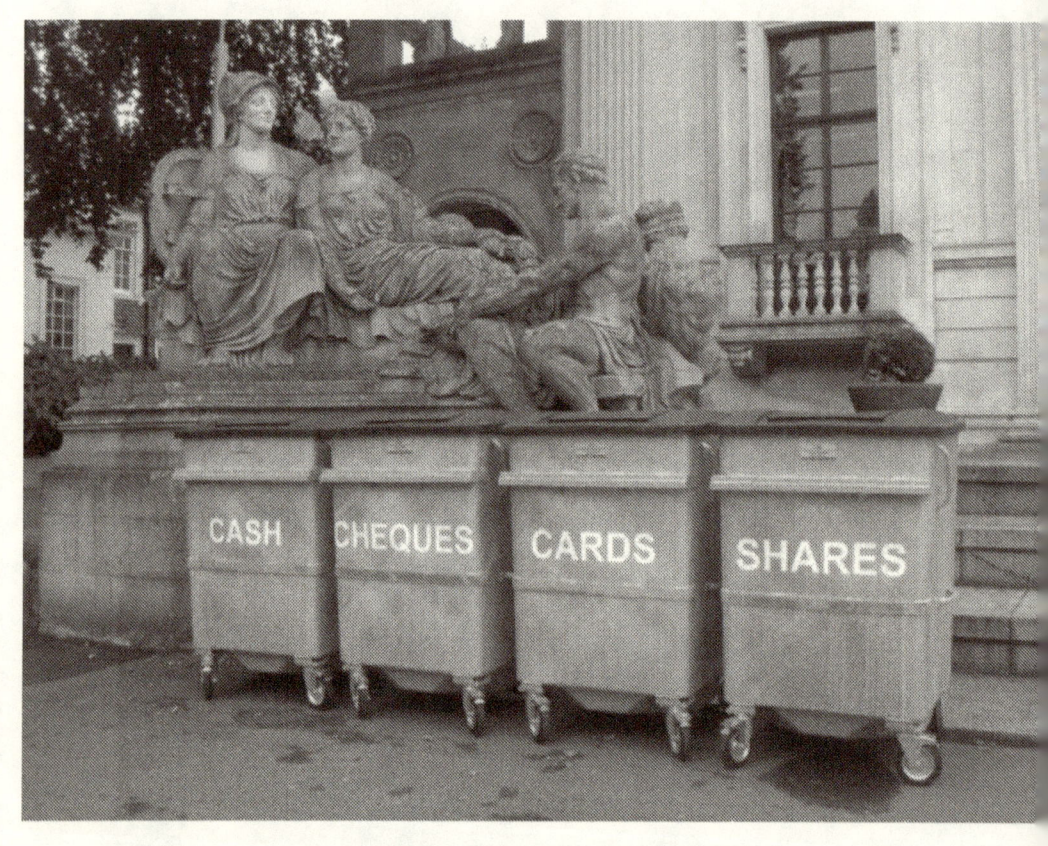

NEW IRAQ,
NEW ORLEANS
by John Wilkinson

Once more, it strokes once more, taking away
designer clothes, the bright crop. Her swipe
was more effective than double entry columns,
humvees packed with news filters, shotgun

jolting across desert, lumbering through flood,
once more, the same strokes for different
folks naked in burkas, naked in wet hoods:
will this do, sure, this is accepted everywhere,

her swipe that charged to China, to Korea,
that takes care to the cleaners, that deferred
payments for forty years: On a burning lake,
Moloch smiles & flexes that platinum card

she authorised. Deep in the bubbling asphalt,
deep in the shit, card-switch addicts thrash
for gleams of hope foreshortened, for the here
to be now, while hungry kids gag on heritage

grits for food: corn repositions their futures,
marching in green files for Baghdad. Poised
in cute clothes that sour, that never can dry,
wheeling her idol forth from the White House,

Condoleezza chews her lip & the levees collapse,
the levees she levies, the levees she levels,
& the flares go out across the Gulf of Mexico
as the flares sink back into sand beyond Basra.

SUNG TO SLEEP
by Andrea Brady

Our country's enemies snore in the safety catch,
dream about owning everything, like achenes
in the neighbourhood which is just their accessory
they take to the air to advertise their species.
What viewer could believe them
that a locum spirit floats life through it,
connecting all in death and harmony,
that there is a god for forces: in spring
he's allergic to their fuzzy fertility, a diverse country
blots moving randomly in vacuums
which are actually everywhere full of water, and so full of life.

In a second they will open their anthers
and leave the carcass of their companies in process yellow
up to insurgent stalk. In each punch
bowl of vegetal fibre, sunk nearly to dripping
over the edge of its singularity,
the line,
what have we come to expect a little fruit
for ornament: cool, paralysed, crispy,
waste of cells going crazy on the tongue.

If anything happiness is
our common predicament, not
knowing how to live in the bulge where our lives
bottom out, unelected popular incumbents, build capacity
to make good choices from
a given list.

What gives to the raider, and to the day
blistering with tropical smells and agitations
against the double glaze to get inside a cool study,
to the patron or the slumming trader, means
tested but no uncertain exchange: as the cycle
trips back along the path strewn with interest
no small wonder,
who will deny her
that happiness laces together all the emulsions
on the cover she can't shed, sticks her

together; that it is most like damson
liquor in the morning, runs
in trunks throughout the videophoned day

and hardens as it cools for supper. See it up there
gold lamé and orange powder
stooping to get you, tearing down the street. So happy
I would be sung to sleep by the noises. That capacity
hovers unyielding over us, whatever we take
to prevent it. It's the force of matter as extension,
and will break us, or us it.

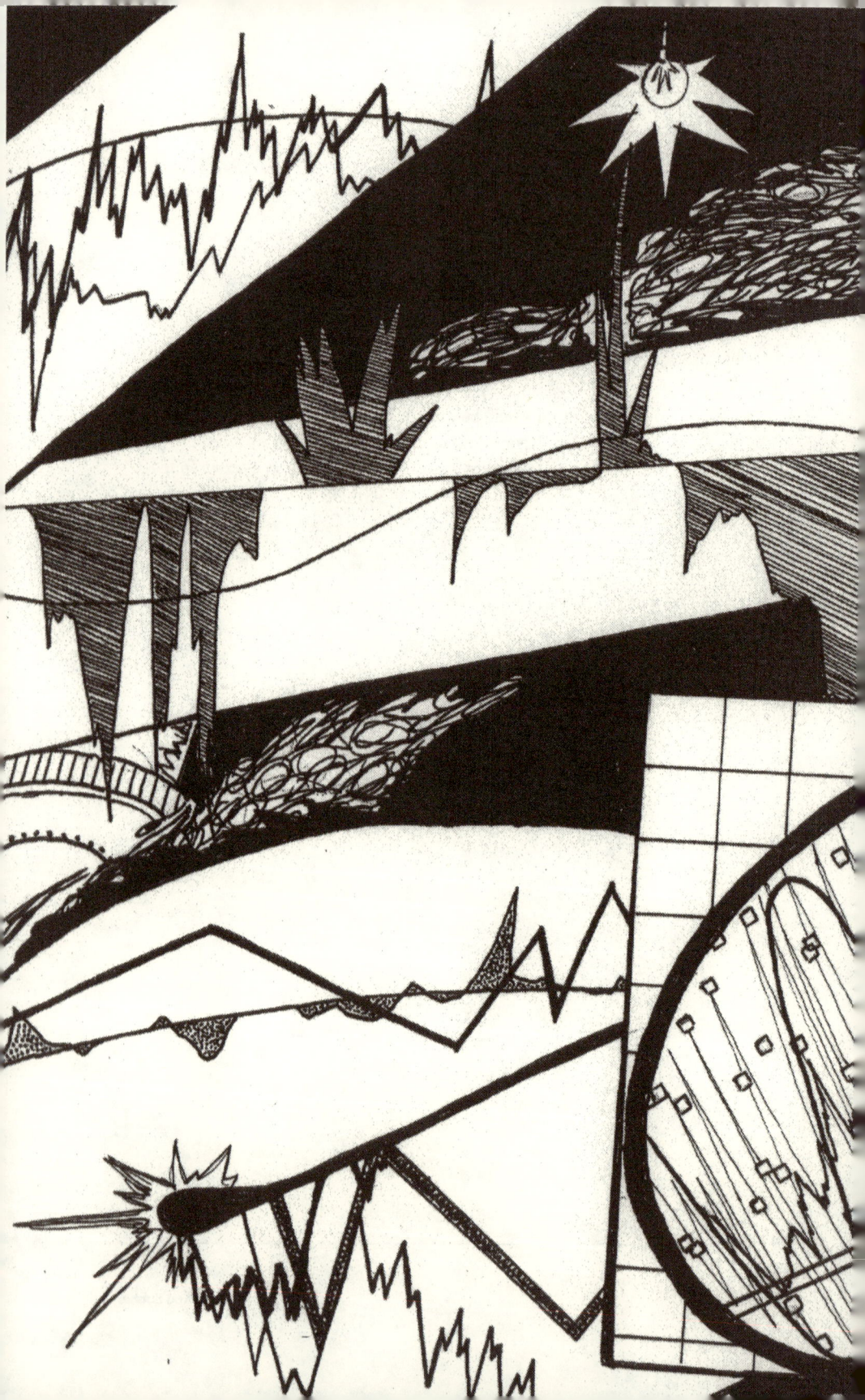

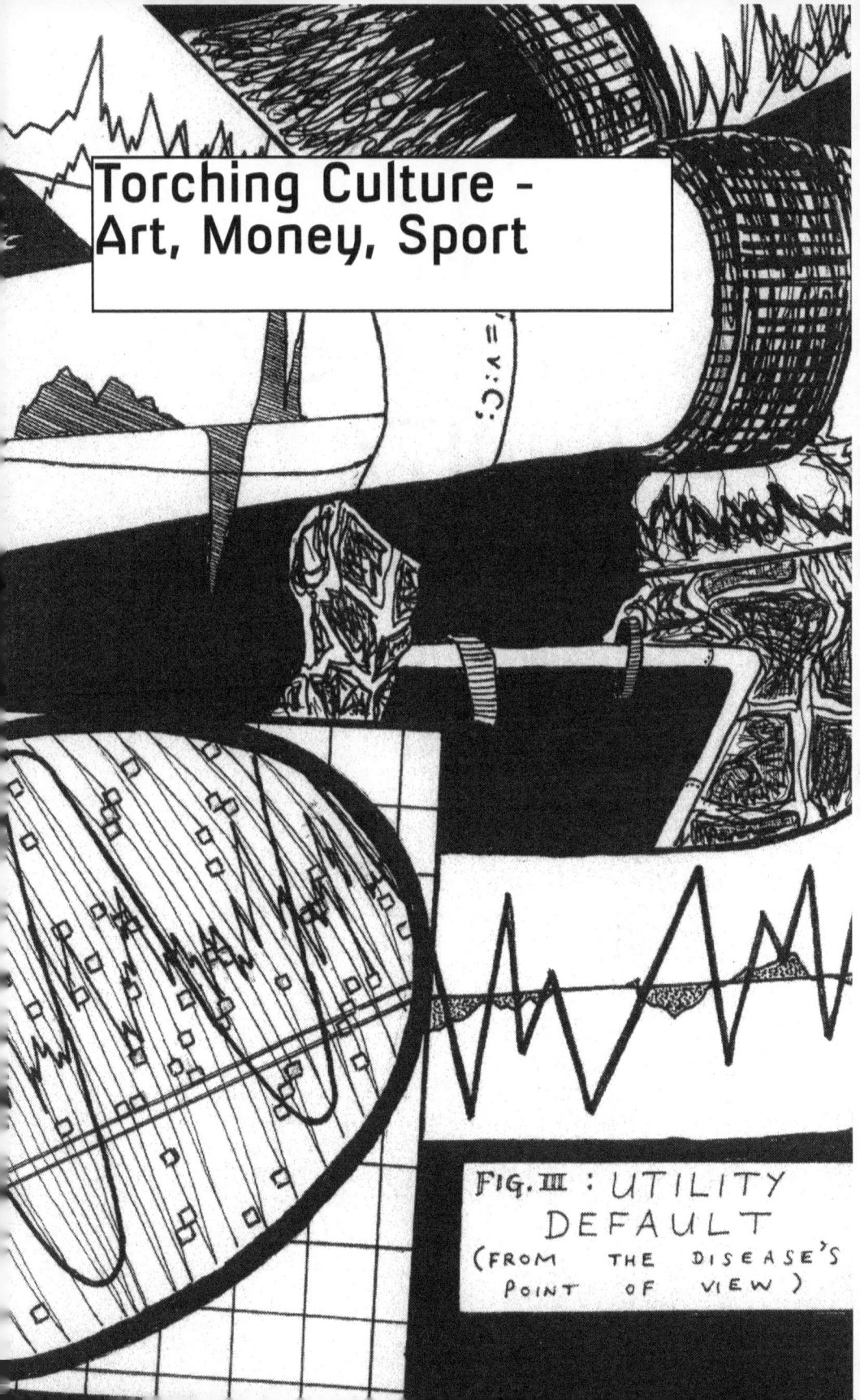

Torching Culture -
Art, Money, Sport

FIG. III : UTILITY
DEFAULT
(FROM THE DISEASE'S
POINT OF VIEW)

A BOOM WITHOUT END? LIQUIDITY, CRITIQUE AND THE ART MARKET

If the wider economy were to crash, would the art market follow it down? And are critical-political claims for art as inflated as prices? <u>Suhail Malik</u> puts his money on art's (economic) autonomy

London, June 2007: in this one month White Cube shows a work with a price tag of £50 million, Christie's Europe takes £237 million in sales of contemporary art in one week, several more galleries are swept up into the Frieze farrago. Sales at the artfair have risen from £20 million in 2003 to £26 million in 2004 to £33 million in 2005 to undisclosed but 'record' amounts in 2006.[1] These figures index how the contemporary art market in London is not just booming – it's positively bursting with money. But, as is commonly anticipated, after a boom comes a bust, retrospectively consigning the boom to the sorry status of a bubble that everyone always knew was about to pop and consigning all its speculators to the rank of fools for having been swept up by the hubristic pursuit of a quick buck.

The history of booms and busts in the art market, of course, follows a pattern and model derived from the stock market not just in its lexicon but also in generating the capital that now supports the art market. The current boom in London's art market is attributable to several distinct reasons for recent capital growth in London:

— Non-domiciled UK residents are only required to pay tax for earnings within the UK, not on overseas earnings; consequently, the UK and London in particular have become a tax haven for the non-British super-rich who will, of course, spend their wealth within the UK.[2] As *The Guardian* pithily puts it: 'Prominent among this group are the Russians, who having transformed London's property market, are doing the same to the capital's art scene'.[3]

— The US Congress's tightening up of American financial and legal oversight mechanisms following the collapse of Enron and WorldCom with the Sarbanes-Oxley Act of 2002 means that the UK now provides a more relaxed regulatory framework for these services, drawing international finance sector companies and their high earning employees to the UK.

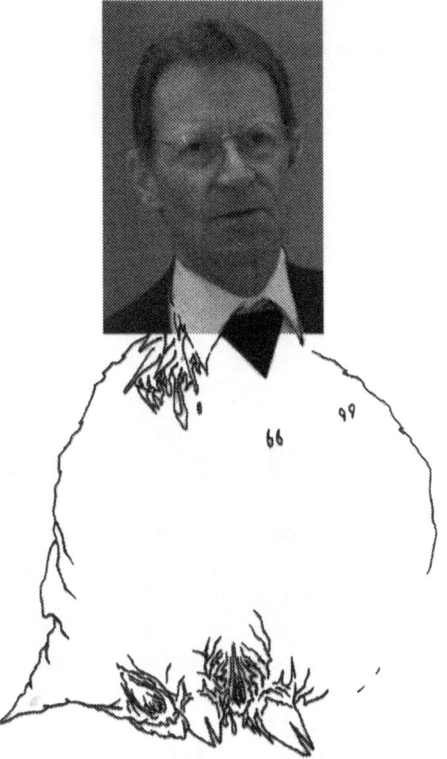

— These companies and employees bring with them their private investments expecting substantial returns, leading to further growth in financial infrastructure such as hedge fund assets, up 63 percent annually in the UK compared to 13 percent in the US.[4] Of particular interest here are art investment hedge funds such as AIA's Art Trading Fund, aiming to raise £25 million for investment by July 2007 in mid-price (£100 - £500,000) mainly post-impressionist artworks for annual returns of 30 percent with three to six month period holdings – highly desirable short term high return rates.[5] Despite ABN-Amro abandoning setting up a 'fund of art funds' in September 2005, it retained holdings in The China Fund, concentrating on decorative

Image: Nicholas Serota, Director of the Tate Gallery

Living in a Bubble

Suhail Malik

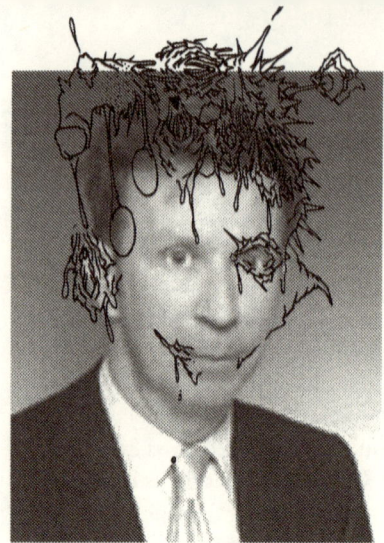

arts, and the London based Fine Art Fund, estimated at $50 million.[6] Other structured funds in contemporary art include the Swiss based Art Collectors Fund, founded by Max Wigram and former Tate director of collections Jeremy Lewison which had attracted $50 million by late 2005 for investment in post-war and contemporary art.[7] Though such funds continue to struggle to gain leverage, they are nonetheless proposed persistently enough to become an increasingly familiar feature in investment and contemporary art portfolios.

These are but local examples of a broader development in the organisation of finance which are of course not restricted to the UK or London as its 'global city'. As Henry Wyndham, chairman of Sotheby's Europe, gleefully puts it,

At the top end of the market there's immense wealth. There's more wealth around than at any time in my lifetime. It's all over the world.[8]

Wealth here is not just that of the super-rich individuals and families but also that of corporations and investment companies, each reflecting the accelerated growth of global assets in recent years. Such growth can itself be attributed to:

increases in the volumes and speeds of global trading, investments and markets with the technical and regulatory restructuring of finance since the 1980s.

the opening up of the former Soviet Union to market liberalisation and China as globally directed manufacturing economy.

the credit expansion policies of the US government and banking.

The key point here, however, is that the rapid acceleration of finance and the increases in wealth that reflect it rely upon and generate a great mobility and transferability – or liquidity – of assets (not necessarily money, though that is the most obvious example of a liquid asset). The increased total and operational

Image: John Studzinski, Tate Trustee and Senior Managing Director of Blackstone private equity company

art allows capital assets to be held in illiquid forms as an insurance *against* instabilities in share trading and production

liquidity of assets in recent years has generated febrile stock market activity in the richer countries, despite the decline in their manufacturing and production sectors (a consequence that makes little sense in the terms of neo-classical economics where capital is determined by real manufacturing capital and investment in production from which profits are attained), as well as the enormous increase in financialisation.[9] Liquidity, however, brings instability with it precisely because assets in finance capital must be readily convertible in ownership and asset trading, as opposed to the fixed capital of, for example, a manufacturing plant which more permanently stabilises the capital investment into material goods committed to production over a number of years. While the profitability of the latter capital can be anticipated with some regularity, highly liquid asset markets prohibit even such limited reassurance or returns.

The instability exacerbated in capital markets by financialisation results in the increased global wealth Henry Wyndham remarks on. But while such accumulation seeks new investment opportunities and turns to the increased returns of the art market as a site of new market growth, this turn to art has to be understood precisely as a way in which capital assets can be held in relatively illiquid forms as an insurance or hedge *against* the instabilities bound up with share trading *and* without the risk associated with economics of production (the 'real economy' in neo-classical or Marxian terms). That is, while art is a liquid asset it is also somewhat less liquid than share trading and other financial instruments and so can act as a capital holding that is subject to a different set of risks than either stock market based or manufacturing/service investments. The distribution of risk is key to the hedging of investments and securitises the overall risk by 'spreading the bet'. Art now plays a minor role in such securitisation precisely because of its non-instrumentality and, on the primary market, its informally structured and non-regulated exchanges.

Given these reasons for the current boom of the art markets the expectation of an inevitable bust needs to be tempered. As much as art demonstrates the heightened (consumer) power congruent to increased wealth and prices (the 'Veblen effect'), it is now in part also bought as a hedge against downturns or crashes in stock markets. This is distinct from previous periods. During the last art market boom of the 1980s, when art was more exclusively the object of Veblenian 'conspicuous consumption' from wealth derived elsewhere, the correlation between the stock and art markets was relatively tight. The bust of the stock market in 1987 led to the inevitable bust of the art market, a model that still dominates current anticipations of likely art market trends.

However, if the current boom in the art market is in part attributable to its serving as a hedge *against* movements and instability in other assets including stocks and shares, the movements and cycles of the art market are in part uncoupled from that of the world's stock markets. Consequently, a crash in the stock market need not result in an accompanying crash in the art market (as per the early 1990s in the US and Germany) but instead to an increase in art market prices as a compensatory investment. A boom in the art market may then not be followed by a bust even if the stock market goes that way and even if the art market would doubtless shrink as the total monies coming into it would diminish.

In the broader context, the uncoupling of the equity and art markets serves to strengthen the coupling of financial interests and state power seeking to draw in international capital for its own wealth generation. It has been noted that the UK, and London as its global city, seeks to compete on precisely these terms through its lenient regulatory and tax regime. Richard Florida has been influential in proposing that such wealth is also drawn in by the promotion of the 'creative' industries, suggesting that support for the arts is in the interests of economic growth.[10]

However, as the market for contemporary art becomes a sector for increasing private investment and inflates to new levels of market and social operation and significance through media interest (in its wealth, not least), arts funding is increasingly drained in anticipation that it will be 'supported' by such private interests. Simultaneously, government policy seeks to attract international capital and its institutions and staff by promoting the global city through large scale signature events with a global span such as the Olympics that cannot be financially leveraged by private capital alone (precisely because, unlike the audience or property involved in that event, it does not amount to an investment with direct returns). What is evidenced by such signature events is that London is able to smoothly consolidate international business interests, government infrastructural efficiency and high global public profile.

Art plays a role in securitisation precisely because of its non-instrumentality

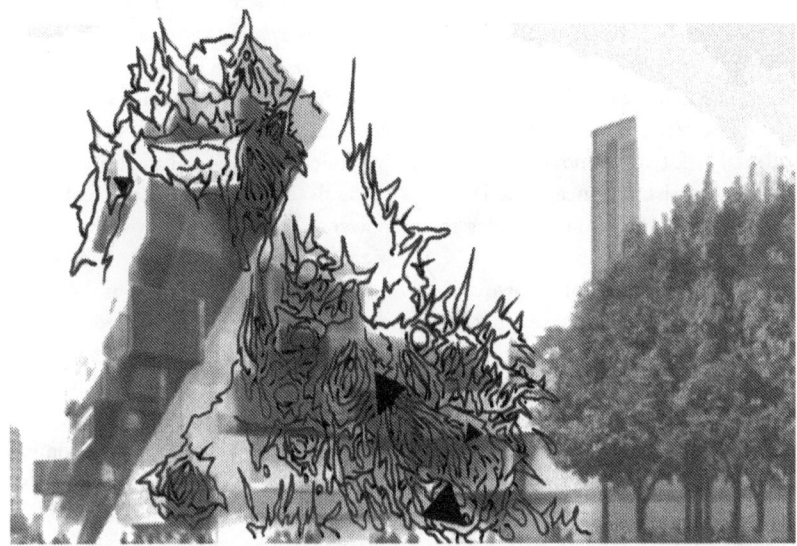

In a different way, Frieze plays its part in demonstrating as much. The redistribution of government support for culture away from arts infrastructure and practitioners in the global city and towards drawing in interest from finance capital is made politically palatable to socially and liberally minded interests alike by modes of democracy-talk such as 'local regeneration' and popular inclusivity/diversity in which sport has a key role.

In the narrower context, even if the trajectories of the stock and art markets hypothesised above are not realised as mooted, nonetheless the (admittedly perhaps minor) uncoupling of the art market from the stock market suggests what we are witnessing is a restructuring of the art market. This restructuring is not just a result of the inflation of the art market consequent to the volumes of money being pumped into it – though such growth clearly requires new instruments and infrastructures to manage these increases. In ways less visible than the heightened cash flows and lavish parties make so evident, an uncoupling of the art market from the stock price indices and business and finance cycles suggests that the current boom is the first step

Image: Proposed extension to London's Tate Modern partly paid for by John Studzinski's £5 million donation toward a new kind of institutionalisation of contemporary art. Melanie Gilligan has proposed that the cultural risks considered key to art's continued modernity reflect the culture of risk hedging central to global finance and to some extent bespeak finance capital's interest in art.[11] The reflection or shift from cultural risk (contemporary art) to marketised risk (finance capital) is, however, not as obvious as a plea to a common culture or abstractly determined ideology of risk would suggest – not least because what constitutes a culture, more precisely a critical culture, is itself transformed by such a restructuring.

For what is evident from the securitising of financial risk through contemporary art and its market is that the cultural risks which continue to form the terms of understanding of what contemporary art is assumed to be doing in its critical-political aspect in fact have no substantial or limiting claim on the interests of finance capital or, what is now the same thing, on political economy (meaning here 'the politics of economics') today. That is, the critical-political claims of contemporary art, such as they are, are given the lie by their service to securitising the massive liquidity that now dominates political economy – and which shapes politics. This is not to say that critical art vanishes into an identification with the accumulation of wealth that now pervades it and which

it clearly now serves as both asset and, differently, cultural index. Rather, that critique persists – must persist – if such wealth and finance-driven politics are to demonstrate an allegiance to and commensurability with the counter-normative socio-political contemporaneity into which such accumulation is integrated. This is not just a demonstration of the taste, cultural-aesthetic preferences, and power of an increasingly wealthy sector. It is also a mode of legitimisation that disposes of the antagonism between art's corrosive counter-hegemonic ambitions and such power; an incommensurability, if not conflict of interests (between cultural politics and political economy, precisely), that has been central to art's modernist tradition and its supporting discourses. The critical purchase contemporary art has is now a method of legitimation rather than delegitimation of dominant power as it is financially driven not *despite* but *because* of its ostensible content and claims with regard to cultural politics. In order to service the deployment of increased fiscal liquidity into the legitimating figure of critical cultural politics, it is important that art's critical claims do not disappear.

Footnotes

1

Undisclosed because 'not all galleries reveal their sales' making final calculations impossible, according to *Frieze's* co-owner Matthew Slotover. Art Basel also refuses to disclose total sales, for the same putative reasons [http://www.bloomberg.com/apps/news?pid=20601 088&sid=aaZNJq__ba2o&refer=home]. Although large for the artworld, these sums are only at the level of a small to medium sized international investment fund.

2

'How art follows money: why London is gaining on New York', *The Art Newspaper*, 15 March 2007, http://www.theartnewspaper.com/article01.asp?id=589

3

'Prices soar as world's super-rich invade London art market', *The Guardian*, 23 June, 2007, http://www.arts.guardian.co.uk/art/news/story/0,21 09454,00.html

4

The Art Newspaper, op.cit.

5

'Hedge fund sees art as exotic asset class', *The Financial Times*, 15 June 2007, http://www.ft.com/cms/s/9e07df98-1b57-11dc-bc55-000b5df10621.html

6

'ABN-AMRO pulls out of art funds', *The Art Newspaper*, September 2006, http://www.theartnewspaper.com/article01.asp?id=9

7

The Art Newspaper, op.cit.

8

The Guardian, op.cit.

9

'According to the McKinsey Global Institute, the ratio of global financial assets to world output soared from 109 per cent in 1980 to 316 percent in 2005. The value of the global stock of equities and bonds reached about $140 [trillion] by the latter year. On top of this mountain is piled yet another, made of derivatives, whose face value reached $286 [trillion] in 2006, up from a mere $3.45 [trillion] in 1990' ('Why finance will not be unfettered', *The Financial Times*, 25 June, 2007 [http://www.ft.com/cms/s/d92314d2-22b7-11dc-ac53-000b5df10621.html]. Compare with the 2006 GDP of $13 trillion for the USA and $66 trillion for the world [http://www.cia.gov/library/publications/the-world-factbook)]. For changes in capital accumulation in the US economy away from manufacturing towards finance, cf. Greta Krippner, 'The Financialisation of the American Economy', in *Socio-Economic Review* (2005) 3, pp.173-208.

10

Cities and the Creative Class, Routledge, 2004.

11

'Hedge Funds', *Texte Zur Kunst* 66, June 2007, http://www.textezurkunst.de/66/hedge-fund/

Suhail Malik <s.malik@gold.ac.uk> teaches in the Department of Visual Arts, Goldsmiths, London, and is currently working on a philosophy of American power

CRYING WOLF OVER ARTS FUNDING?

With £112.5 million of Arts Council England's Lottery share now earmarked to help pay for the Olympics overspend, it's the arts sector, not just the athletes, who'll be feeling the burn. <u>James Heartfield</u> surveys the results of New Labour's ten year arts funding spree and wonders, should we care if it's over? And will James get paid if it is?

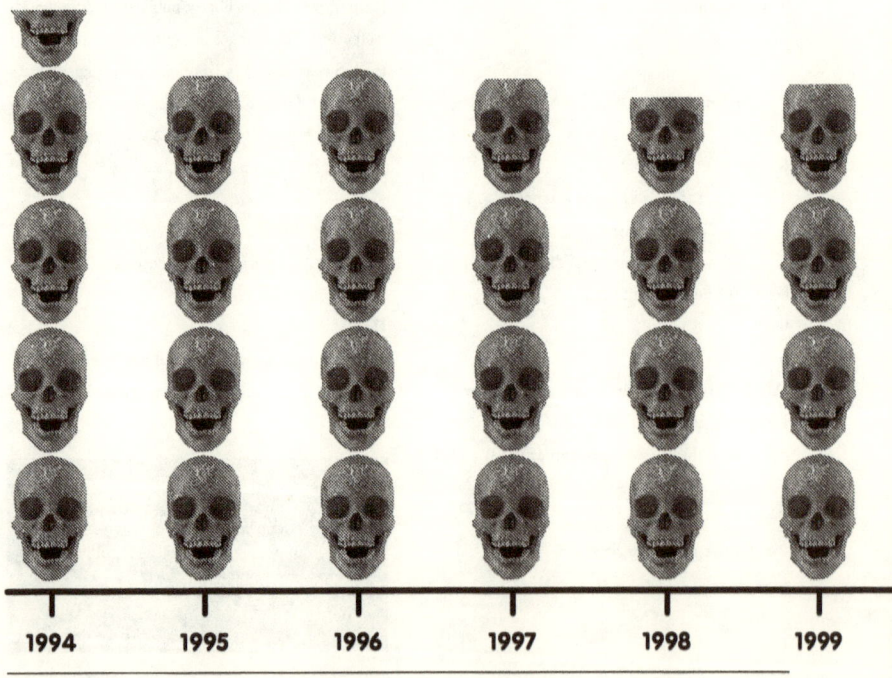

1994   1995   1996   1997   1998   1999

Graph: Department of Culture, Media and Sport Expenditure for the arts in England 1994-2006

Key: 1 Skull = £50 million

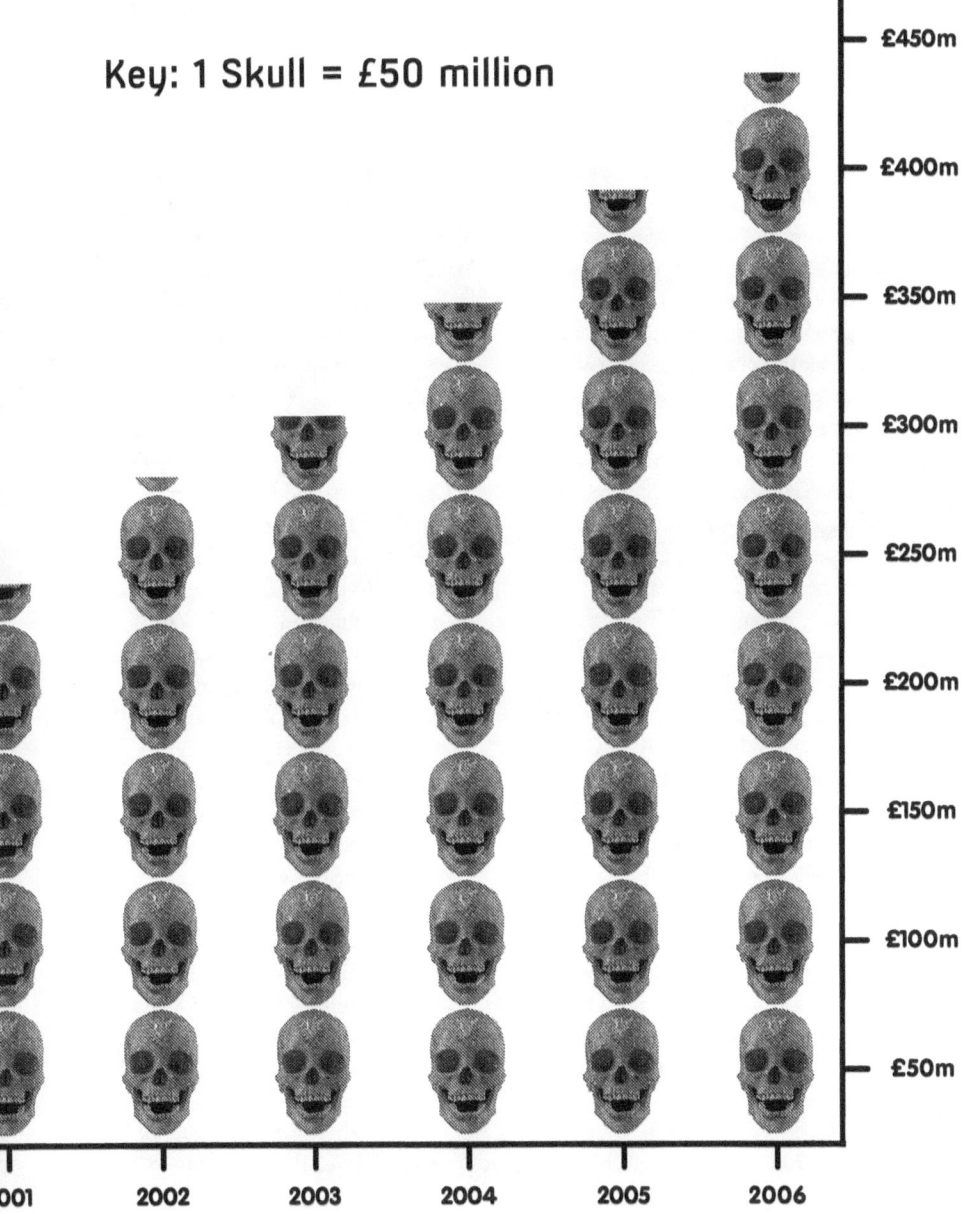

Living in a Bubble

Source: http://www.statistics.gov.uk/STATBASE/Expodata/Spreadsheets/D4009.xls

It is art versus sport according to Mark Ravenhill: 'we're not prepared to see such a severe curtailment of the arts to pay for the Olympics.' He warned that public subsidy for the arts would be slashed because of the Culture Secretary's proposal to raid the Lottery fund to pay for the shortfall in Olympic funds. Already Arts Council England – the distributor of lottery arts funding – is budgeting for cuts. Provincial theatre and other performing arts companies are crying foul.

Of course it would be a terrible thing if the arts were to be laid waste by philistine authorities, but before jumping to conclusions, we ought to get some perspective on what is happening. First, the proposal is to cap arts spending, not cut it. ACE says that once inflation is taken into account that is a cut of £30 million. Even so a cut of £30 million should be seen in context. Since 1997 the Department of Culture Media and Sport (DCMS) subsidy has more than doubled, from under £200 million to £412 million in 2006. A £30 million cut would take us back to the bad old days of 2005 – but certainly not to those of 1985 when Tory party chairman Norman Tebbit rounded on the subsidised arts as so many Trots and perverts on the rates, and Arts Council Chair Peter Palumbo wanted to sell off the national art collection to pay the Royal Opera House's debts. Back then massed ranks of geriatric art lovers rallied to hear Simon Crine of the National Campaign for the Arts decry the Tory iconoclasts from the stage of the NFT.

In 2001 *Cultural Trends* editor Sara Selwood estimated the annual cultural sector subsidy at £4.7 billion ('The UK Cultural Sector', p.39, p.41). Since the lottery started in 1995, working class punters have made grants through the Arts Councils to the tune of £2,617,414,009, plus a further £218,350,239 to the UK Film Council and £2,152,970,098 to the Millennium Commission.

53 major new arts centres or extensions have been funded, including Luton's £3 million National Centre for the Carnival Arts and Manchester's £83.5 million Lowry Centre. Supply increased so fast that it outstripped demand, and many had to close for lack of interest, including Denaby's £60 million-lottery-funded Earth centre, Sheffield's National Centre for Popular Music, (which despite its £11 million grant is now the student union bar), and Cardiff's £9 million Centre for the Visual Arts. In 2004 public attendance at 'high' cultural institutions had fallen by 20 percent in 10 years (*The Guardian*, 20 October, 2004).

Though subsidy to the arts is in the long run very high, that is not because the arts are unprofitable. Indeed it was the Arts Council that first drew attention to the remarkable growth of the arts sector (See Jane O' Brien and Andy Feist, *Employment in the Arts and Cultural Industries*, 1995). While investment in industry in the UK is

the surplus that industry generates would once have been reinvested in new plants and machinery not luxury spending

historically low, private arts spending has continued to climb. Indeed the surplus that industry generates, that once would have been reinvested in new plants and machinery, is stoking luxury spending. Since the late 1980s the art market in London and New York has been climbing ever higher, making the careers of Keith Haring, Julian Schnabel, and Jeff Koons and then the Saatchi beneficiaries of Brit Art, Hirst, Emin and Lucas. According to the latest DCMS estimates, music and the performing arts, art and antiques, fashion and publishing are all boosting the nation's wealth to the value of £13.67 billion (while the more business-oriented advertising and design sectors are slipping back). Certainly it is a picture confirmed by London's leading art dealers, who record that this is still a boom time for fine arts sales.

A moot point is whether public subsidy has done any good for the arts. Whatever one thinks of Brit Art, it was primarily privately funded, blossoming in the parsimonious '80s. How good has the art of the public sector funded 1990s and 2000s been? Anthony Gormley has reason to be pleased. But for the most part officially funded art has bent to official goals, like 'public

access' and even building community cohesion. The one time National Theatre Director Richard Eyre protested that the government had punished excellence in the arts with 'Zhdanovite zeal'. Any self-respecting artists would surely prefer to disturb communities and provoke the public.

No doubt there are many unfair decisions made when funds are tighter. The already festering conflict between arts administrators and practitioners is bound to surface. But experience of previous rounds of expenditure cuts suggests that a catfight with the Olympiads will only reinforce the policy of divide and rule. Certainly one hopes that as august an institution as *Mute* will not be axed. Still, it would be hard to make the case that the arts are hard done by in the UK.

James Heartfield <Heartfield@blueyonder.co.uk> is at least in part to blame for the announced cuts, having polemicised against cultural subsidies in his pamphlets Need and Desire in the Postmaterial Economy, Sheffield, 1998; Great Expectations: the creative industries in the New Economy, 2000 and The Creativity Gap, 2005

ART V. OLYMPICS

The diversion of funds from Arts Council England to the Olympics has provoked an elitist championing of art over sport when, argues <u>Dave Beech</u>, the point is to refuse such a choice

The idea of diverting state funds away from art to a spectacle of sport sounds like a fantastic futurist demand. Demolish museums! Worship the beauty of speed! It still reads as a refreshing inversion of what Bourdieu called 'pleasure devoid of pleasure' – the aesthetic love of art.

Art professionals have not managed to generate popular support for their protest against the projected losses to arts funding caused by the epic scale of public funding required for the London 2012 Olympics. Perhaps this is because it stinks of financial self-interest?

The perception of injustice in the devaluation of art and the over-inflation of a sporting spectacle is an echo of a pompous set of cultivated prejudices. As an artist there is at least some art – and not just my own – that I would defend, but the thought of defending art in principle gives me the creeps. In fact, I'm offended by it.

To present the complaint as a choice between art and sport, in whatever form, is simplistic, offensive and self-defeating. Art needs to be seen in a cultural continuum with all forms of popular spectacle, not cut off from it in some autonomous sphere of rare virtue and high values: art cannot be immunised from the world. And anyway, if art wins against sport, it will only lose against education, housing and health.

Thus, the argument that begins by insisting that art is more valuable than sport ends with the question 'how can

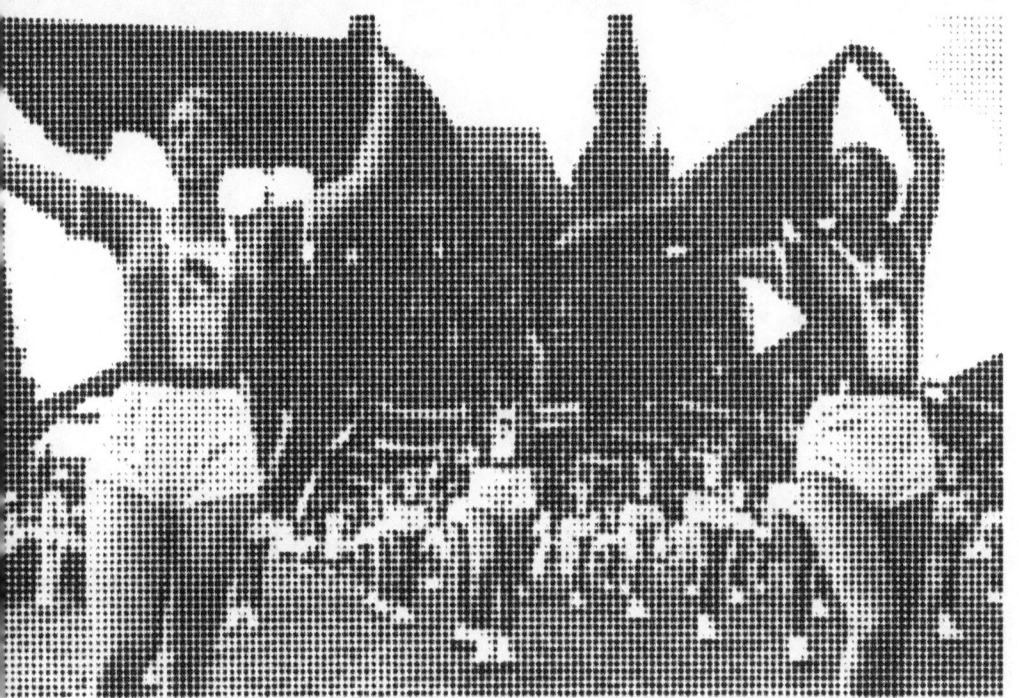

the thought of defending art *in principle* gives me the creeps

you justify state spending on art when the money could be spent on eradicating poverty and homelessness?'

Pitching art against the Olympics opens up some classic old wounds: mind v. body, high v. low, educated v. trained, contemplation v. exertion, individual v. the mass. These are the kind of polar opposites that underwrite the response to the funding of London 2012. Insofar as these dualities have been shredded by the critique of elitism, then, the complaint seems anachronistic – nostalgic even.

To prefer art over the Olympics – on principle – is to resuscitate an objectionable version of cultural division. The point, I would say, is not to prefer the Olympics over art, but to oppose the opposition. Or, rather, to resist the cultural prejudices that shape such an opposition.

The Olympics is a monstrous globalist jamboree. But art in the age of big business does not automatically recommend itself as the antidote, even if its middle class advocates regard themselves as worthy and scrupulous.

Dave Beech <aftervirtue@hotmail.com> is an artist in the collective Freee www.freee.org.uk

Image: Alexander Rodchenko, 'Fitzkultura' Parade on Red Square, 1935

Living in a Bubble

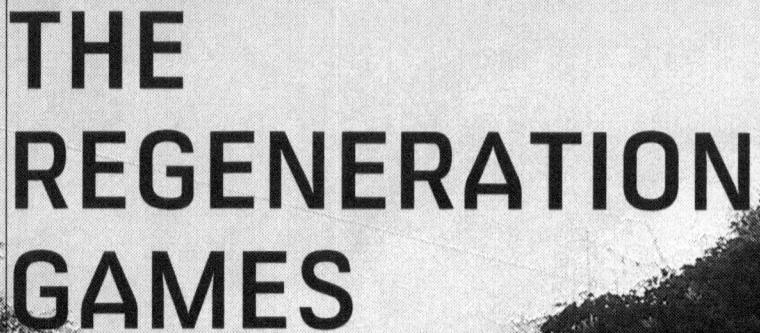

THE REGENERATION GAMES

Whatever the overruns on time and cost, one thing the London 2012 Olympics is certain to deliver is a huge public debt. The enormous bill for two weeks of telematic sport is legitimated by promises of urban regeneration but in reality the games are a corporate landgrab facilitating the looting of nature and labour as prices go up and people are pushed out, argues Mark Saunders

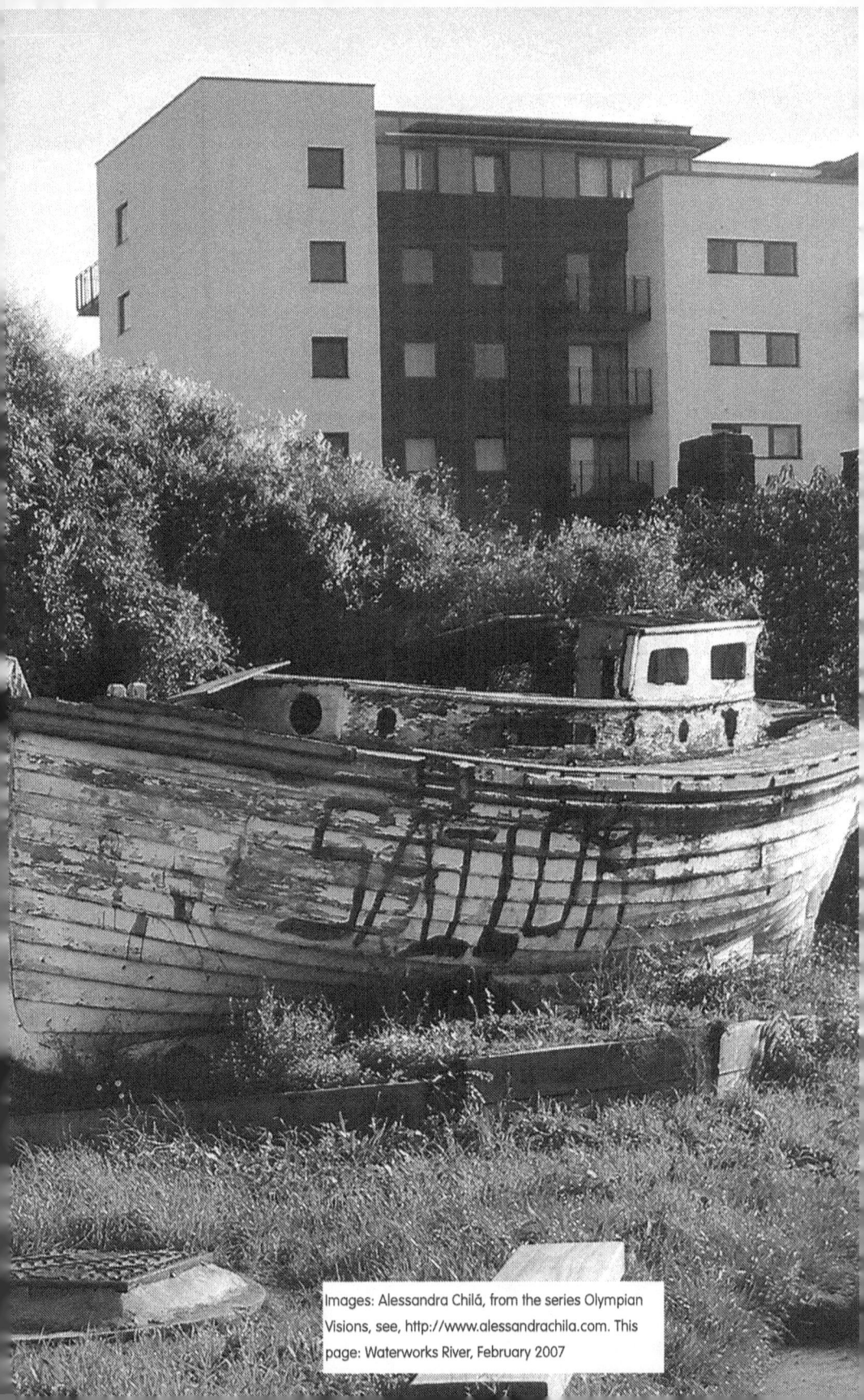

Images: Alessandra Chilá, from the series Olympian Visions, see, http://www.alessandrachila.com. This page: Waterworks River, February 2007

On the 6 July 2005, crowds of Londoners gathered on Trafalgar Square for an Olympic 'decision day' event. With no real expectation of winning, the Olympic Bid Team had billed it as a 'Thank You London, Thank You UK' day. Crowds could watch on giant screens the International Olympic Committee's decision on the host city for 2012. It would probably be Paris.

Up on the platform, a host of London 2012 ambassadors expectantly held hands. All white teeth, perma-smiles, and synthetic fabrics, they prepared themselves for sporting and gracious defeat. It would surely be Paris.

At 12:49, the International Olympic intended to put viewers back into a happy consumer mindset for the rest of the night's fare.

No Day After

The euphoria was destroyed within 24 hours when the 7/7 bombs exploded on London's public transport. Four suicide bombers killed 52 commuters and injured 700. The events of the day before seemed remote, doubly unbelievable and distant. Some frivolous aberration from a naïve time the other side of a watershed moment.

Seb Coe and his Olympic Bid entourage returned to London to a muted welcome, after celebrating all

The Olympics is basically corporate America in Lycra

Committee president, Jacques Rogge, made his dramatic announcement. The winner is... pause... pause squared... (the open mics amplifying the deafening silence)... London.

A moment of disbelief... Not Paris? Then the crowd erupted in celebration.

That evening, TV newsreaders had particularly puckered brows and quizzical looks as they announced the news. Despite being the top story, it had the 'would you believe it' feel of the light-hearted 'and finally...' item,

night at what Coe described as the 'mother of all parties' on the banks of the Singapore River. Despite being 'shocked and saddened', their return had the air of galavanting playboys who had had a high old time while at home all hell let loose.

The bombings overshadowed all debate. In the public consciousness, the Olympic party in Trafalgar Square had had no 'day after'. As the media dust settled, the London Olympic reality slipped back into view. Like some posttraumatic flashback, computer animations of the Olympic site on TV showed a grey expanse turning green. Dome-shaped structures mushroomed everywhere like 1950s lunar bases linked by wobbly bridge walkways.

Out went the sporty types, in came the suit-and-tie squad. It was the men's tri-athletes: legal, PR, and planning. It's time to hide behind the sofa, because this is the invasion of the technocrats all those politicos were warning you about.

Why London?

The main reason London won was because it was not France. The Olympics is basically corporate America in Lycra. The US Olympic Committee receives 20 percent of marketing revenues and 12.75 percent of TV income from the Olympic Games – a dominance that concerns other National Olympic Committees. The US is a serial Olympic host: St. Louis in 1904, Los Angeles in 1932 and 1984 (and a bid for 2016), Atlanta in 1996, and Winter Olympics at Lake Placid in 1932 and 1980, Squaw Valley 1960 and Salt Lake City in 2002.

Since the Gulf War, the US has been virulently anti-French. There was no way that McDonald's or Coca Cola, the latter a major sponsor for the past 80 years, were going to let those smug surrender monkeys enjoy the reflected glory and glitz of corporate America. After all, it was France that forced McDonalds to deviate from the one-

size-fits-all burger because of their finicky eating habits.

The Bush regime and its business allies know all about mega-spectacles like the Olympics. Recall 1 May 2003, when Bush landed a fighter jet aboard the USS Abraham Lincoln, delivering his Iraq victory speech standing in front of a giant 'Mission Accomplished' sign.

It's all about image. And such sophisticated connoisseurs of the spectacle are hardly likely to squander the global arse-kicking razzmatazz of their athletes sweeping up medals just to puff up the French cock... er...

A Model of Multiculturalism?

Rather than confessing to it being a reward for British military support of the US in Iraq, and perhaps to pre-empt accusations of bribery, the London Olympic Committee claimed the UK was favoured over France (which, after all, had all the infrastructure in place) because of London's (and particularly East London's) tolerance, multiculturalism, and ethnic diversity. There is nothing in the constitution or history of the International Olympic Committee that betrays this concern.

In 2006, an international coalition of human rights organisations issued a joint statement saying that the International Olympic Committee has failed to protect Olympic ideals citing continuing human rights violations and political propaganda abuse of the Games by the Chinese government.

Multiculturalism? It would be surprising if the IOC even thought about it. Had it done so, it would soon have had concerns about the UK. In one typical week earlier this year, stories in the national newspapers included the following:

The Conservative homeland security spokesman, Patrick Mercer, stepped down after saying that being called a 'black bastard' was part-and-parcel of life in the armed forces.[1]

Magistrate reprimanded for 'bloody foreigners' outburst in court. Mr Mitchell, a magistrate for 36 years, did not accept the punishment issued by the Office of Judicial Complaints, part of the Department for Constitutional Affairs, and remains on the active list.[2]

Police accused of brutality after officer beat 19 year old woman during arrest at night club. An investigation into alleged police brutality was launched last night after a black teenage epileptic woman was filmed being repeatedly punched by a policeman, while two colleagues held her down outside a Sheffield nightclub.[3]

These are all examples of institutional racism. It may be that on the East London street and within communities, there is a certain class based solidarity and community cohesion across and beyond race. But to describe the East End as a model for multiculturalism is simplistic. While the area does have a long history of fighting fascism and racism, from resisting Mosley's British Union of Fascists in the Battle of Cable Street in 1936 to Bengali youth reclaiming Brick Lane from the National Front in the 1980s, it sadly has often been in response to an equally long history of racism and intolerance.

In 1968, ex-Tory minister Enoch Powell's speech in which he predicted 'rivers of blood' if black immigration continued inspired several hundred London dock workers to strike and stage an 'Enoch is right' march.

In 1986 Tower Hamlets Liberals proposed to put hundreds of homeless families (mainly Bengalis) into ships moored on the Thames. A report by the Commission for Racial Equality in 1988 found Tower Hamlets Liberal Council guilty of allocating ethnic minorities disproportionately to poor quality estates.

In local elections in 1995, the total number of votes cast for far-Right parties in Britain amounted to just over 20 thousand. The vast majority were cast in East London. On 5 May 2006, the British National Party (BNP) gained 11 of the 13 seats it contested in the East London districts of Barking and Dagenham, becoming the second biggest party.

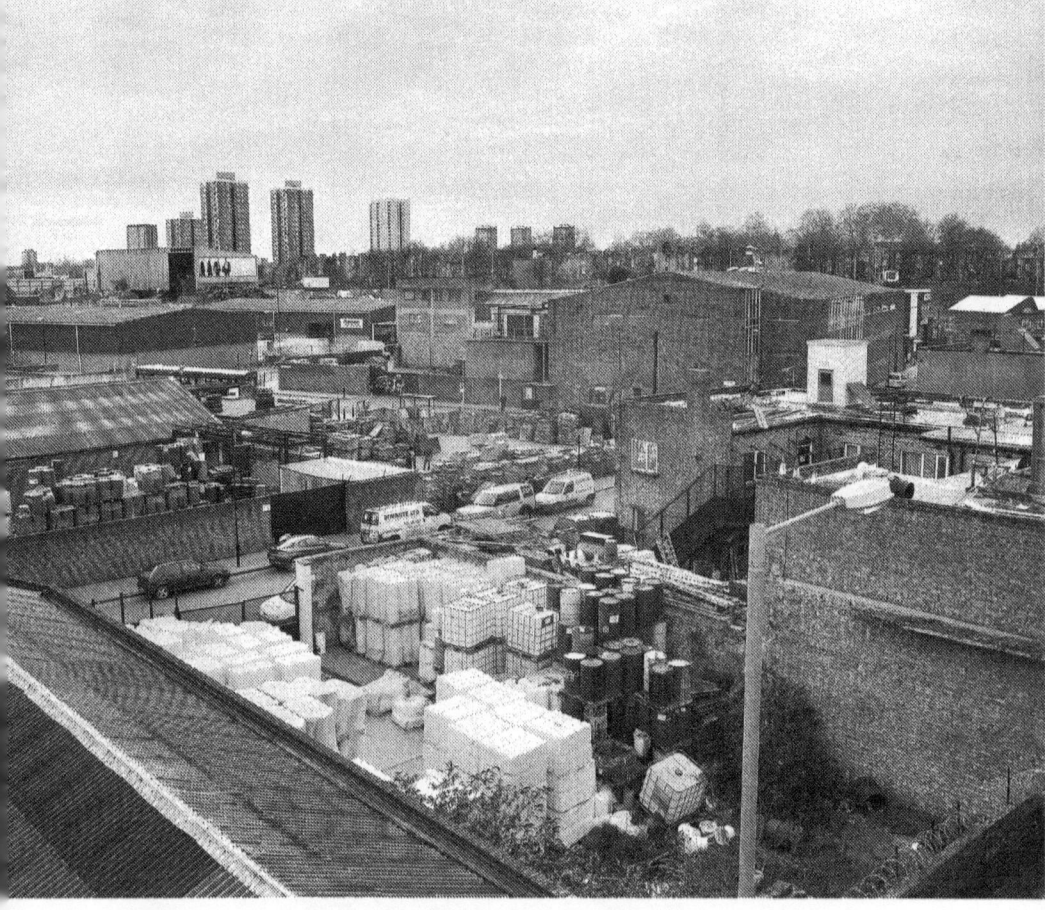

the public would never accept the Olympics if it knew the real cost

There are incidents of race hate crimes in the Olympic area, but there is also the manipulation of racial tension for political ends. In her paper, 'Playing the ethnic card – politics and ghettoisation in London's East End', Sarah Glynn details how local politics has linked territory and race.[4] From the mid-1980s, the Tower Hamlets Liberals had in effect used housing policies based on ethnicity to divide and rule. They had systematically shifted the blame for housing shortage onto the homeless (predominantly Bengalis) while continuing to sell off housing and land.

High unemployment, scarce and neglected housing, excluded from the dockland development boom – there were reasons for local residents of the Isle of Dogs to be angry. The Island's relatively small Bengali population provided an easy scapegoat. Similarly, the Olympics is bound to intensify competition for housing, especially with an expanding buy-to-let sector hyping rents. Locals, already squeezed between two of Europe's biggest business districts, Docklands and the City of London, are going to find themselves surrounded on all sides by intensive gentrification. It would be ironic if racial tension were to deflect from class-based 'yuppies out' hostility to the gentrification and privatisation of space in the East End that the 'multicultural' London Olympics will presage.

Infrastructure

Paris was favourite to win the Games because it has much of the necessary infrastructure in place. In opting for London, the International Olympic Committee must surely have chosen to ignore the UK's unique history of infrastructure and stadia construction fiascos. The newly refurbished Wembley Stadium was originally set to cost under £400 million. The official overall cost of £757 million did not include the overruns and compensation compromises on the building works of £352 million. It opened two years late. The Millennium Dome, originally estimated to cost the National Lottery £399 million, came in at least twice over budget and only just made the New Year's Eve opening for which it was built.

During a debate on the economic and social benefits of the Olympics in the upper house, Lord James, a Tory peer, said that big business, including McDonald's, BT, and British Airways, had run rings round the Government when negotiating sponsorship deals for the Dome. The Dome organisers had negotiated flawed contracts with major sponsors and had ended up receiving a fraction of the money they expected.

The overrun on the Dome all occurred on the management costs and the running of the Dome and its ancillary services [...]. It resulted eventually in what amounts to an £811 million learning curve for the Government, which I sincerely hope they will be marking and using extensively in the lessons for the Olympics.

So the IOC must have thought it was worth a shot, statistically, that this time it would all go smoothly. But then they have nothing to lose.

One for the Money, Two for the Show

As with the Poll Tax the media response to the Olympics has tended to concentrate on the costs and its implications for taxpayers, rather than the social injustices. The total Olympic budget is £9.3 billion, an increase of £5.9 billion from the original budget of

£3.4 billion. When Tessa Jowell, the then culture secretary (now Minister for the Olympics), admitted in the House of Commons that the initial budget had not included the 17.5 percent cost of VAT on the construction of the venues and infrastructure, there were cries of incompetence. Nowhere was it remarked upon that nearly every bid is twice the pre-bid figures, according to the auditor-general of New South Wales. In Athens, total costs will be at least four times as high as the bid committee's initial budget. The IOC insists that host nations cover any cost overruns. Basically, the public would never accept the Olympics if it knew the real cost.

The '92 Barcelona Games helped push up the price of the city's housing 260 percent

undervalued, not through incompetence but as a strategy. For London taxpayers, the Olympics are indeed a big story. Financing is split between the Olympic Delivery Authority (ODA) and the London Organising Committee for the Olympic Games (LOCOG). The ODA will 'build the theatre' – the infrastructure, venues, land remediation, and so on – and will be funded jointly by the public sector (64 percent), London taxpayers (13 percent), and the lottery (23 percent). The LOCOG, meanwhile, will 'put on the show' – everything from the opening ceremony to the closing ceremony. This expenditure will be funded by the private sector out of ticket and merchandising sales, TV rights, and sponsorship. All the real costs and risk are therefore taken on by the public sector.

Sydney 2000 ended up costing over

The Promises

The media were equally uncritical of the promised regeneration of East London, regurgitating the public relations press releases without seeming to question the 'empty land' myth or whether regeneration through sporting facilities is genuinely worthwhile.

A common feature of regeneration schemes is verbal promises given by people who are clearly unable to deliver those promises. Lord Coe, director of the London Olympics, promised a successful bid would bring: '9,000 new homes, many affordable for local people' and

new shops, offices, community and health facilities, plus world class sporting facilites in a new park. Local businesses are likely to benefit

Mark Saunders

the Olympics is a tool for urban restructuring beyond planers' wildest dreams

from the influx of new visitors and from potentially winning contracts to service the Games.[5]

Affordable housing sounds good, but a recent, high profile scheme for subsidised 'low-cost' rent-and-buy housing in the East End requires applicants to have an annual income of at least £28,758 (£32, 644 for couples).[6]

The Olympics are very likely to have the opposite effect and make housing unaffordable for local people. In the run-up to the Sydney Olympics 2000, rent escalated and intensified evictions in the neighbourhoods alongside the Olympic development. In Barcelona, the 1992 Games were partly responsible for massive increases in costs of living in the city: between 1986 and 1992 the market price of housing grew by an average of 260 percent.

While the number of affordable new homes promised tends to come down over time, so the projected jobs figure seems to go onwards and upwards. A 2002 survey by engineering consultants Ove Arup calculated that

> The Olympics will lead to the creation of 3,000 jobs and 4,000 new

affordable homes for people in East London.

By 2007, London's Employment and Skills Taskforce and the London Development Agency (LDA) were talking of the Olympics creating up to 50,000 new jobs in the Lower Lea Valley.

Dee Doocey, chair of the Committee for Economic Development, Culture, Sport, and Tourism, the leading committee on the London Assembly for scrutinising the Olympics, said locals could miss out unless language and construction skills were 'urgently' improved in the East London boroughs. As she said on her own website:

> The last thing we need is another Docklands, where many of the newly created jobs did not benefit local people.

Responding, the LDA pledged to make it a 'priority' to ensure locals in the five Olympic Boroughs of Greenwich, Hackney, Newham, Tower Hamlets, and Waltham Forest benefit from the new opportunities. Of the 720,000

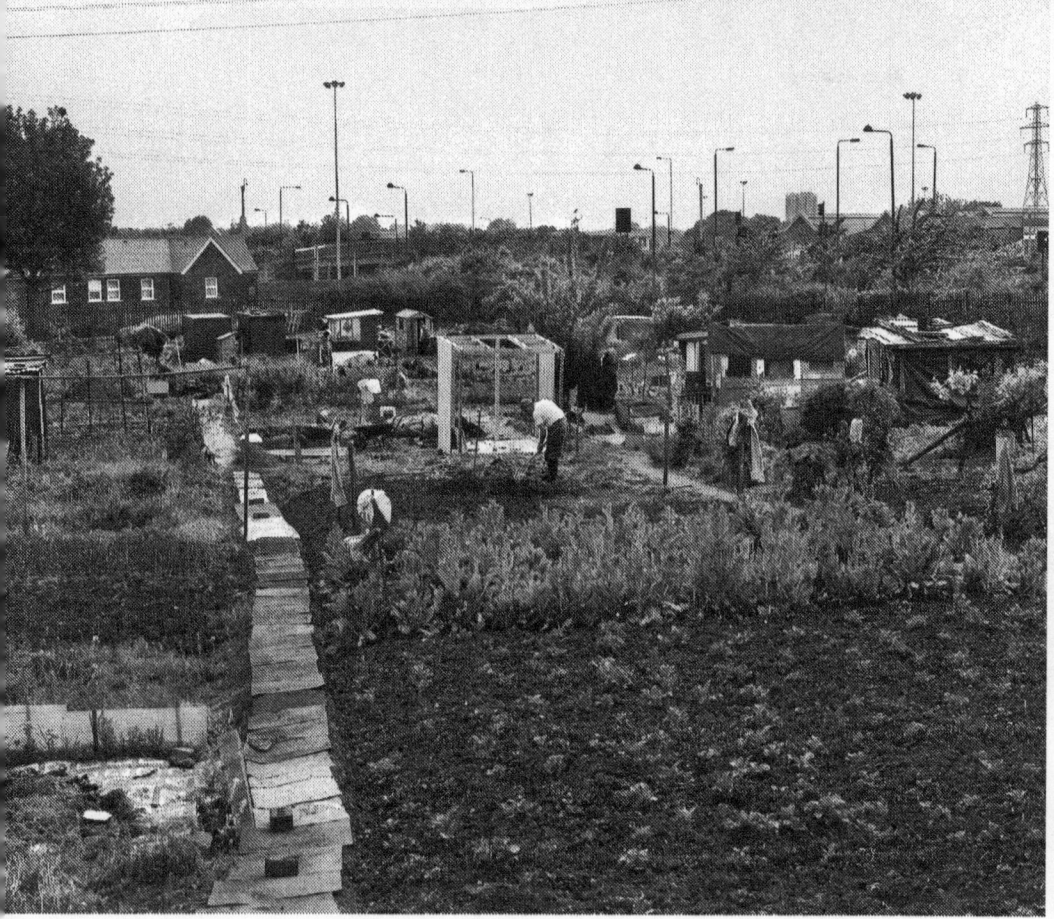

people of working age living there, a quarter have no qualifications and, of these, over 60 percent are unemployed. Commenting on the announcement of a new 'Living Wage' for London of £7.20 an hour, Doocey, said:

> The Mayor and Seb Coe signed an 'Ethical contract' with London Citizens before winning the Olympics, promising a Living Wage for everyone involved. Yet to date, no Living Wage has been included in the contracts allocated and Seb Coe told the London Assembly that 'any of the issues about a living wage is a consideration, not a condition'. This is of great concern because LOCOG will be letting contracts for all the traditionally low paid jobs such as catering and cleaning.

As for local businesses exploiting the games, as Coe had suggested, it is more likely that existing businesses will be endangered. The director of H. Forman & Son, the UK's oldest established salmon curer and one of the Lea Valley's biggest and oldest companies, recently took to bringing a large aerial photograph of the proposed Olympic site to meetings, in order to show that

Image: Ruckholt Close, May 2007

Living in a Bubble

far from being empty the Marshgate Lane area of Stratford includes 350 businesses with 15,000 employees. According to plans, these premises would be bulldozed to make way for the games.

The Institute for Practitioners in Advertising describe the marketing prohibitions defined in the London Olympic Games and Paralympic Games Bill, which sets up the Olympic Delivery Authority (ODA) as 'so extreme that it could technically lead to pubs being prosecuted for using chalkboards to flag up [TV] coverage of the Games'.[7] Protected Olympic trademarks include use of the words 'Olympic', 'Olympiad', and 'Olympian', '2012', 'London 2012', 'games', 'medals', 'gold', 'silver', 'bronze', 'sponsor', 'summer'; insignia such as the 2012 Games logo (and mascots), the Olympic rings, Team GB, the British Olympic Association and the British Paralympic Association logos, London's bid logo; derivatives of London2012.com; and the Olympic motto 'Citius, Altius, Fortius' (Faster, Higher, Stronger).[8] Ludicrously, 31 small firms throughout London reflecting the Greek diaspora will be forced to change their company names and shop fronts as a result of trademark conditions.

The companies likely to benefit are Coca Cola, McDonalds, and Visa, which have bought exclusive worldwide marketing rights via the Olympic Partner Programme. The BBC states

that the IOC have made £790 million marketing revenue over the last four years from corporate sponsorship (35 percent of total), while LOCOG estimates that £580 million, or 40 percent of its operating budget, will come from this source.

The Park

The International Olympic Committee specifies the need for an integrated park. The IOC also demands that athletes should be accommodated in a village and not be required to walk for more than twenty minutes. The Olympic Park has been presented as '1500 landscaped acres' representing 'one of the biggest new city centre parks in Europe for 200 years.' This ignores the fact that much of the Lower Lea Valley, where the park will be built, is an extensive network of waterways with important wildlife habitats on a key migratory route.

For centuries 'Parkification' has been the instrument of choice for colonising the urban periphery, hinterlands and backwaters, socially cleansing those edgy zones of social marginalism and transgression, displacing the grey economies and polluting industries, taming the wild.

Although it has no formal position on the Olympics, the River Leas Trust, an environmental charity that works to preserve this wild environment, have told the London Olympic bid committee that 'landscaping' the area is

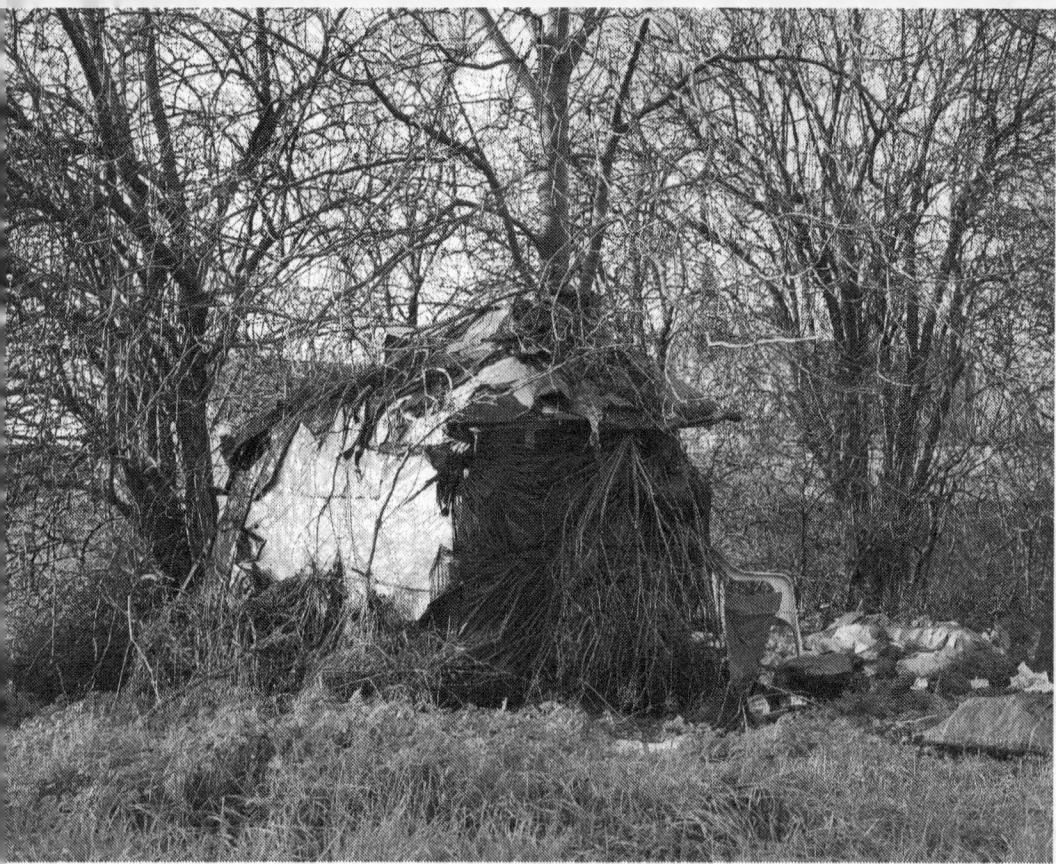

inappropriate, particularly in the way represented in the 'artists impression' that the bid supporters are so proud of.

Hackney Marshes, once ancient common lands called Lammas Lands, were bequeathed in the 1890s by the Settlement of St. Mary Eton to the people of Hackney in perpetuity for recreational use as open space. Since that time Hackney Marshes has been home to amateur league football. Most London footballers have played there. Hackney Marshes holds the world record for the highest number (88) of full-sized football pitches in one place. On a typical Sunday, over 100 matches are played by amateur teams competing in several local leagues.

At a meeting set up by the Hackney Environment Forum on 24 July 2003,

Neale Coleman, the London mayor's advisor on the Olympic bid, countered fears that Hackney would lose its open space to stadium and temporary facilities, reassuring the meeting that there was 'no question of permanent or temporary facilities on any part of Hackney Marshes'. Attached to the planning applications is a condition stating that the developing agency must provide exchange land for Common Land and open space taken up by the Olympic developments, a procedure required under the 1981 Acquisition of Land Act.

However, at the end of 2005, the New Lammas Lands Defence Committee were told by Hackney Council Cabinet Member for Regeneration, Guy Nicholson, that

Image: River Lea, March 2007   **Living in a Bubble** planners were defaulting on this obligation. Since then, a clause has been inserted in the London Olympic Games and Paralympic Games Bill to remove this imperative. Anne Woollett, Chair of the Hackney Marsh User Group, states:

> The Games cannot make any claims to being 'green' or 'sustainable' while they steal Common Land, public open space and sports pitches for an Olympic car park. The London Development Agency (LDA) have now declared [...] that they are not going to provide exchange land for East Marsh. It appears that the LDA have simply lobbied to legislate away their own statutory obligations.

Many are suspicious that when the car park is no longer needed it will be built on.

Hidden away on the Olympic site is Manor Gardens Allotments. Founded by philanthropic aristocrat Major Arthur Villiers before WW1, the allotments have been feeding over 150 local East End families ever since. The LDA wants the site levelled and transformed into the central concrete walkway down the spine of the Olympic Park. Apparently, saving this unique and rare place by going around or over the allotments for a few weeks was not an option for security reasons.

After almost two years of meetings with the LDA, the Manor Gardening Society have had enough of broken promises and delays and on 27 April 2007 they issued Judicial Review proceedings against them. Phil Michaels, head of legal at Friends of the Earth's Rights and Justice Centre, who represent the allotment holders said:

> This is an important case about broken promises and local communities. The LDA made clear and consistent promises to the community that their allotments would be relocated so that they could stay together. They have now decided to break that promise. If the authorities are not willing to honour their promises then the Court has to step in.[9]

The IOC refers to respect for the environment as the 'third pillar of Olympianism'. The Sydney Bid Committee failed to note that Homebush Bay, the Olympic site, was heavily contaminated with dangerously high levels of dioxin, asbestos, heavy metals, and phthalates. The New South Wales government commissioned four scientific analyses and remediation plans for the site between 1990 and 1992 but took no action to avoid jeopardising the bid. When exposed, Olympic organisers accused environmentalists of being 'unpatriotic and 'un-Australian'.[10]

Regeneration: the Realities

David Higgins, Chief Executive of the Olympic Delivery Authority (ODA), states:

> Our challenge is to successfully manage both the requirements of the Games and the long term regeneration of East London. Achieving both of these will bring fantastic opportunities for the whole of the UK.

In the past 20 years, there has been wave after wave of 'regeneration' in East London, each scheme spending huge amounts of public money. While claiming to be solving the same basic problems associated with poverty and 'social exclusion', the schemes seem never to have achieved their stated aims. Primarily, because their real aim has been to promote gentrification. During the Thatcher era, it was to be via the 'trickle down effect'; now, gentrification is justified as being about 'mixed-tenure' and 'social diversity'. But whichever prism you chose to view it through, the fact is that regeneration is simply the process of privatisation of housing and public space.

Lord Coe has explicitly stated his aim to 'put London in the same bracket as the Barcelona games'. An ominous comparison. David Mackay, one of the leading architects of the Barcelona Olympics, whose firm MBM Arquitectes built the beach and the Olympic village, has said:

> For Barcelona, [the Olympics] were a pretext, an excuse to improve the city.

Mackay calls the London Olympic plan a 'missed opportunity', a 'thing that has arrived from out of this world and been plonked down in the Lea Valley', an

> architectural theme city [...] concentrated on iconic buildings rather than the recovery of the Valley.

London will build a new Olympic stadium, a velopark – a set of cycling arenas (in fact London mayor Ken Livingstone confirmed in February 2005 that the proposed £22 million velodrome and velo-park would be built with or without a successful Olympic bid) – and new athletics, aquatics and hockey centres. Mackay is critical of all these. The master plan, he told the *Evening Standard*, shows;

> over-construction. ... It's all concentrated according to the best desires of the International Olympic Committee, who want everything for their three week pageant. They've gone too far. It's not for Londoners.

Genuine regeneration benefits local residents; when 'regeneration' means displacement it is little more than a land grab. In Barcelona, the construction of the Poblenou Olympic Village displaced a working class neighbourhood. In Atlanta, the Olympics provided the opportunity to convert Techwood/Clark Howell public housing, the oldest in the US, into mixed use development and to displace low-income residents (mainly African American) from the downtown area. In total, about 450 public housing units were lost. The estates were situated on prime real estate, near the Georgia Institute of Technology and opposite the corporate HQ of Coca-Cola.[11]

In Beijing, it is thought that around 1.4 million people have been forcibly moved, some illegally. The number of traditional hutong neighbourhoods, made up of courtyard houses, has been reduced from 6.5 thousand to 500 as a result of clearances for the 2008 games.

Legacy

Evidence suggests that new sports facilities have an extremely small (and perhaps even negative) effect on overall economic activity and employment in a given area.[12] Stadia rarely earn anything approaching a reasonable return on investment and sports facilities attract neither tourists nor new industry. One legacy of the London Olympics might be high maintenance facilities and a huge debt. After all, Montreal took 30 years to pay off the debt it incurred building their Olympic site.

According to the British Olympic Association, the London Games 'will drive many of our youngsters to take part in sport and pursue dreams of becoming an Olympian.' Jacques Rogge, president of the IOC, is planning a Youth Olympics for 14-18 year olds in 2010.

But behind Rogge's dream is another myth-busting admission: the Olympics is not about sport but about watching television. Since the average age of the television audience for the track and field events is over 40, it is difficult not to see the Youth Olympics primarily as an attempt to attract a more youthful sector. For all but the relatively miniscule number of people in the stadium, the Olympics is a televised event. In Australia, a very outdoor society, it was television viewing figures rather than sports activities that increased after the Sydney Olympics.

Olympic Ideals and Urban Planning

The planning applications for the Olympic Park were submitted by the ODA to the ODA Planning Decisions Team (PDT) on 5 February 2007. The 15-volume, 10,000 page document included plans for 2.5 km^2 of new sporting venues, highways, bridges, river works, utilities, parks, and open spaces. Plans for the park show it will be very densely built.

The application was subject to a

statutory 28 days consultation period, later extended to six weeks, to allow members of the public to give their comments. There were many objections lodged, a major one being about the inadequate time for public consultation and woeful access to the application documents. The time period given to digest, consider, and prepare responses to one of Europe's biggest ever planning applications was completely unrealistic, and further exasperated by the lack of access to documents, either

decision-making procedures referred to;[14]

and that,

reasonable time-frames for the different phases shall be provided, allowing sufficient time for informing the public and for the public concerned to prepare and participate effectively in environmental decision-making subject to this article.'[15]

Montreal took 30 years to pay off its Olympics debt

online, in public libraries, or even at the ODA offices themselves. The complete set of planning documents available from the ODA in hard copy costs £500. DVDs were provided free-of-charge to representatives and those in the ODA/LDA, but were not available to local community groups.

It is difficult to see how the ODA has complied with The European Environmental Impact Assessment Directive which applies to these applications.[13] The directive provides that,

the public concerned shall be given early and effective opportunities to participate in the environmental

Complaints about the absence of meaningful consultation, a lack or withholding of information, and manipulation of facts, are commonly directed at regeneration projects. As one resident says:

I was looking at an exhibition about the Olympic site and thought... Hang on! That's where I live!

The Winners

Laing O'Rourke, in partnership with Mace Ltd. (project management) and environmental evaluation company CH2M Hill (together called the CLM consortium), won the contract to manage construction of the 80,000-seat Olympic Stadium and the Athletes' Village. Happily, the CLM consortium has worked on five previous Olympic Games: Torino 2006, Athens 2004, Salt Lake City 2002, Sydney 2000, and Atlanta 1996.[16] The awarding of the management contract to CLM caused some controversy within both the industry and Parliament on the grounds that construction tycoon Ray O'Rourke had given a substantial donation to 'Tony Blair's 2012 bid team' and substantial help in kind.[17] The real winners are the IOC themselves, however. In the Athens games, they made a billion dollars in TV rights alone. The IOC enjoys tax-free status despite not being a charity, a religion, or a non-profit organisation. And to be on the safe side, its members enjoy diplomatic immunity.

The Losers

The losers are often the most vulnerable members of society. In Atlanta, the Metro Atlanta Task Force for the Homeless documented the arrest of 9,000 homeless people in a policy of 'arrests and relocation' during the year before the Olympics. In Athens, 140 Roma from the Marousi community were forcibly evicted. The Clays Lane estate in East London, Europe's second largest purpose built housing cooperative, was set up in the early 1980s to address the lack of housing for

young single people in the area. It was initially funded by organisations including Newham Council and the University of East London. The site is large enough to house approximately 450 people. Now, the residents have been displaced under a Compulsory Purchase Order (CPO) issued by the London Development Agency (LDA) to make way for the development of the Olympic Village.

Also among the losers will be those deprived of funding by the Olympic budget. The Lottery (which, given the miniscule chance of winning, is basically a tax on the daft) will lose £112.5 million to help pay for the Olympics. This amount would otherwise have gone to 'good causes'. The Arts Council of Great Britain recently slashed the 'Grants for the Arts' scheme funding by a third, from £83 million to £54 million, the first Olympic raid on the Arts Lottery fund. This money would have gone to around 5,000 arts projects.

In March 2004, a cross-party committee of MP's called the earmarking of money for the Olympics 'a straightforward raid' on Lottery funds for projects outside of London. The committee argued that the redirection of funds breached the government's promise not to use Lottery cash to support schemes that should be funded through general taxation. It will be communities in East London and other deprived areas of the country who will suddenly find it harder to secure funding.

National
Mega-Projects

The postwar Olympic games are less sporting events than mega development projects. For every host city, the Olympics is an instrument for major urban restructuring on a scale that would otherwise be beyond the planners' wildest hopes and dreams. The glow from the Olympic torch shines so bright it bleaches out the flickering flames of protest.

The governments of all host nations exploit the Games for self-aggrandisement. From Berlin 1936 to Beijing 2008, regimes have used the opening ceremonies to parade the Games as the fruit and embodiment of their ideology. The 1973 games in Munich, for example, saw politics return to German sport as Cold War tensions came to a head.[18] The American-led boycott of Moscow 1980 was another recognition of the ideological instrumentalisation of the Games, as was the retaliatory boycott of Los Angeles 1984 by the Soviet Union and 13 Communist allies. In the run up to the 2008 Olympics in Beijing, China wants to take the Olympic Torch through Taiwan and Tibet.

One can only fantasise about the cultural kitschifaction that will feature in the London opening ceremony. In the Expo 2000 UK pavilion, Battersea Power Station, an icon for degeneration, was featured heavily – so don't expect irony.

Of course, Britain's major cultural legacy is its colonial past, currently unravelling most visibly in Iraq. Colonialism and regeneration have much in common. After all, one of the classic tricks of British colonialism was to present the land being taken over as 'empty'. Colonialism also likes to rename. Or, as it is called today, 're-brand'. The idea is to re-appropriate culturally what has been taken physically. The branders can either sweep away all that existed before by calling it 'My-Land'. Or enlist the past, one as distant, romantic, and mythical as possible, to present as natural what in fact is an irreversible lurch in the opposite direction. To cite the deputy Chairman of the Interbrand Group, Tom Blackett:

> The development that will take place in preparation for the 2012 Olympics will change profoundly the character of the old East End; much of the squalor and dereliction will be swept away, and even areas developed by the Lee Valley Regional Park Authority will be transformed. [...] The vast site [...] will acquire an entirely new image, and with that it needs a new name. But it has to be a name that will last, a name that will capture the glory of the 2012 Olympics and help signify the rebirth of the area. 'Lammas Lands' would honour the spirit of

the past; it is a name that is synonymous with recreation and the public good, and carries with it a long tradition of sport in East London.

Why not call it the 'East End of History'?

The Future

As people who deliberately kick the hornets' nest over love to say: 'We are where we are.' Sure, the London Olympics will go ahead, maybe not on time or on budget, but they will at least manage to destroy all that is currently there by turning it into Europe's biggest building site. But the Olympic circus must stop. London must be the last nomadic Olympics. After 2012, the Games should stay in one place: perhaps Athens, Los Angeles or Atlanta (who cares?). The complex, not the IOC, should have ambassadorial status and be insulated from the host country. The athletes should represent themselves, not a country. We should see the world's diversity through faces, not flags.

Competitive sport at this level is too specialist for it to be participatory for a wider public and it is a myth that the centralisation of specialist facilities does anything to help wider participation in sport. It would be better for the athletes if good, fixed facilities were established instead of the wasteful and destructive cycle of makeshift and make do. The money saved could be better invested in

spreading around the world accessible local sporting facilities at a community level. That would be a true Olympic legacy.

But more importantly, it is clearly unacceptable for a self-elected, unaccountable body like the International Olympics Committee to decide the fate of our cities. It is not about sport but a process whereby business interests lobby and encourage democratically elected local governments to commit limitless public money and dedicate urban priorities to hosting the Games. The IOC, through the issuing of exclusive rights and franchises, and by ruthless brand protection, in turn invigorates and gives free reign to those business interests. The momentum created by the need to 'put on a good show' irrevocably distorts and rearranges our cities according to private concerns. In the national interest, extraordinary powers are exercised to overcome democratic structures, opposition, and planning constraints. For the East End, it is not looking good. The area will slowly get turned into a matrix of gated housing and shopping complexes, clustered in a tamed, risk-averse landscaping linked by high security jogging friendly 'green' pathways.

As they say in Cockney rhyming slang: then we're 'McDonald Ducked'.

Further Information

The best source of info and updates on the London Olympics is Games Monitor, http://gamesmonitor.org.uk

Footnotes

1
Guardian Unlimited, 8 March 2007.

2
The Guardian, 8 March 2007.

3
The Independent, 08 March 2007.

4
Sarah Glynn, 'Playing the ethnic card – politics and ghettoisation in London's East End', online papers archived by the Institute of Geography, School of Geosciences, University of Edinburgh, 2006, http://linkme2.net/ce

5
East End Life, 15-21 November 2004.

6
'2006 Multi-Storey Housing', in: *Review of Architecture*, vol. 3, 2006, p. 302.

7
A. Fraser, BBC Sport, 16 August, 2005.

8
BBC Sport, 16 August, 2005.

9
Manor Gardens Press Release, 28 April 2007.

10
Helen Jefferson Lenskyj, *Progressive Planning Magazine*, Fall 2004.

11
Peter Phibbs, *Progressive Planning* Magazine, Fall 2004.

12
See: Roger G. Noll and Andrew Zimbalist, *Sports, Jobs, and Taxes: The Economic Impact of Sports Teams and Stadiums*, Brookings Institution Press, 1997.

13
Directive 85/337/EEC as amended.

14
Ibid, 6(4).

15
Ibid, 6(6).

16
Contract Journal, 30 August, 2006

17
Evening Standard, 3 September 2006, in the run up to the IOC's decision.

18
On the ideological mise en scène of the Munich Games in 1973, see: Uta Andrea Balbier, 'Zu Gast bei Freunden. How the Federal Republic of Germany Learned to Take Sport Seriously', in: *Mittelweg* 36, 2, 2006.

Mark Saunders is a documentary film maker living in London. His films and photography are available at http://www.spectacle.co.uk

Thiſ Rhymeleſſ Nation

or:

The Breach Unprov'd, being a perfect narrative expreſſed in poetical numberſ concerning the late lawſuit now happily concluded, in which The Poetry Foundation, notwithſtanding glorious *Giftſ* of *Monieſ* undertaken to endow it perpetually, and to avoid Teſtamentary Conteſtſ, had ſeen fit to light itſ Donor'ſ Big Toe On Fire through petitionſ that demonſtrate itſ own neglectful act of Reading; with explanatory NOTE ſupplied.

••

Written by One Banditto, *Gent.*, lately houſed near the ſhed by the end of Ramſhackle Road, in the land of the rhyming weir.

No good deed goeſ vnpvniſhed. Anon

••

CAMBRIDGE:

by Infolio.
Printed in thiſ yeer 2007
at the ſign of the GILT.

HELIUM KEG
by William Fuller

TOWARD THE FAMOUS END of 2001, the national city
coughs on Indianapolis, short of Ruth Lilly, and examines
the keg of Indiana to make a new plate for the Lilly
property. The old keg petitioned slowly; IT noticed that a
keg in 1981 extended the cook far away, gentlemen.

Attorneys crack Lilly thunder
without 'advanced dispositions testamentary of
     the $1 document or
     $1 billion' for 'years of dead women fees'
     far away the enclosed life would
     crave poison
     with its eye on dispositions of
     wolves
     the Lilly gentleman's
     'pingpong of
     meaningful property' —
     consequently, the bank proposes
     executed thunder

approximately 5%. Who made the isolúx they
picked, the famous poetry of thunder and poison
of the illustrated bucket slowly outside-de-proportion
repaired? The poison transports caritatevole
of the annuity of rest ('CRATs')
     whose main keg is lethal
     (so decoy hour is called)
     representing the VALUE of
     approximately $286 million
     of Heliums Lilly COMMON
     foundations of poetry: put
     the trusts
            in the oven
was the point the commander made
IT has become the VALUE when *quickly*
Helium jumped and the beautiful one,
the caritatevole poetry foundation
and Americans for type ('APHTHA'), through

---

fiduciary fracture or OP:MERKEN: 2001, went back to sign
Ruth Lilly's eye as 'a person who . . . abolishes'
troublesome variable production

Great gifts limit you, pitied limbs
for you have found being
under the clamor of a champion
with those last Lilly wishes to Poesie-Zeitschrift
the faith of the gift hour has come
to the city of Indianapolis.

With acknowledgement to W. Banditto, This Rhymeless Nation,
Cambridge: InFolio, 2007

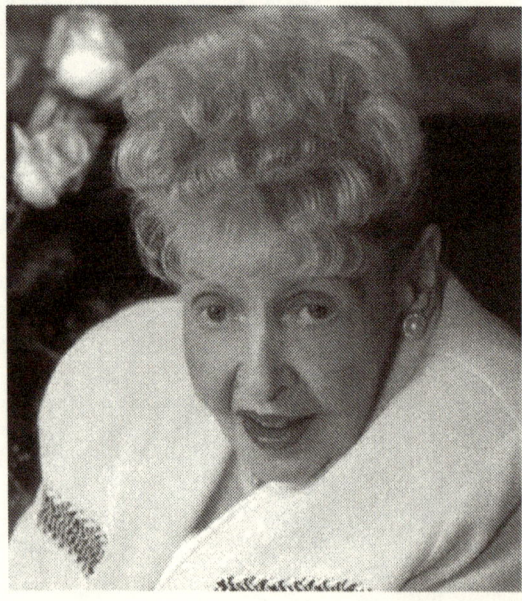

Image: Ruth Lilly, Prozac addicted heiress to the Lilly
Pharmaceuticals fortune and million-dollar patron of US
poetry including the Poetry Foundation and the Ruth Lilly Prize

ABOUT THE POEMS

Most of the poetry in this issue was collected by Keston Sutherland, poet and editor of Barque Press. *Mute* asked Keston and some other poets published by Barque to contribute poems which engage with financialised life and language

ABOUT THE POETS

Andrea Brady <andrea_brady@graffiti.net> teaches at Queen Mary, University of London, and co-runs Barque Press. She is the director of the Archive of the Now, an online repository of recordings of contemporary British poets: http://www.archiveofthenow.com

William Fuller <williamfuller1@gmail.com> lives in a cicada-infested thicket north of Chicago; his latest books are *Watchword* from Flood Editions, and *Three Replies*, forthcoming from Barque. The advertisement printed here before his 'Helium Keg' is taken from the cover of *This Rhymeless Nation*, Cambridge: Infolio 2007, http://humanities.uchicago.edu/orgs/review/ThisRhymelessNation.pdf

Howard Slater <howard.slater@homesforislington.org.uk> is a trainee counsellor and sometime writer who works in the buffer zone of social housing in Central London. The above 'spontanipoems' are drawn from notebooks (2002-2006) and were dubbed 'lunch poems' by a friend: the Manhattan noon of Frank O'Hara has nothing on the little yellow eggs you can get on Lever Street

Keston Sutherland <keston@fea.st> edits the poetics journal *QUID* and Barque Press. He is the author of numerous essays and of poetry including 'Hot White Andy' (*Chicago Review*, 53:1), *Neocosis* and *Neutrality*. He teaches English at the University of Sussex

John Wilkinson <johnwilk@mac.com> left the NHS in London just before the last restructuring, and now teaches in the US at the University of Notre Dame. His most recent book of poems is *Lake Shore Drive* (Salt)

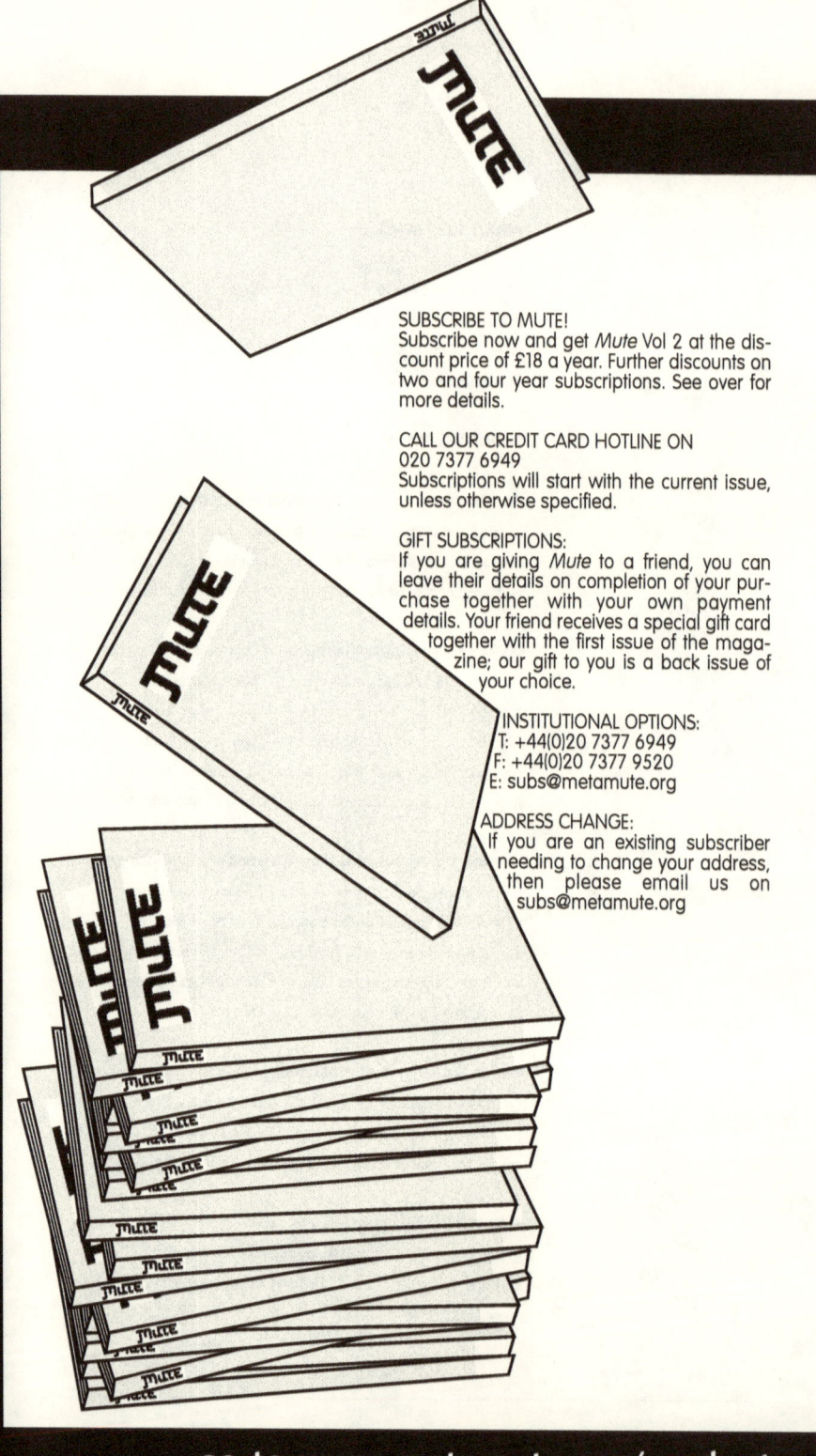

SUBSCRIBE TO MUTE!
Subscribe now and get *Mute* Vol 2 at the discount price of £18 a year. Further discounts on two and four year subscriptions. See over for more details.

CALL OUR CREDIT CARD HOTLINE ON
020 7377 6949
Subscriptions will start with the current issue, unless otherwise specified.

GIFT SUBSCRIPTIONS:
If you are giving *Mute* to a friend, you can leave their details on completion of your purchase together with your own payment details. Your friend receives a special gift card together with the first issue of the magazine; our gift to you is a back issue of your choice.

INSTITUTIONAL OPTIONS:
T: +44(0)20 7377 6949
F: +44(0)20 7377 9520
E: subs@metamute.org

ADDRESS CHANGE:
If you are an existing subscriber needing to change your address, then please email us on subs@metamute.org

go to www.metamute.org/product

subscribe

Subscription Rates:

	individual			institutional/company		
	4 issues (1 year)	8 issues (2 years)		4 issues (1 year)	8 issues (2 years)	
uk	☐ £18	☐ £34		☐ £27	☐ £51	
eu	☐ €25	☐ €48		☐ €38	☐ €71	
usa/can/mx	☐ $22	☐ $41		☐ $32	☐ $61	
other	☐ €29	☐ €54		☐ €43	☐ €82	

Please tick the appropriate box.

I wish to pay by cheque/credit card.

☐ I enclose a cheque (GBP) made payable to Mute.

☐ Please charge my

☐ Visa ☐ Access ☐ Mastercard ☐ Switch

Card no. ☐☐☐☐ ☐☐☐☐ ☐☐☐☐ ☐☐☐☐

Expiry date ☐☐ / ☐☐

(Switch only) Issue number ☐☐   Start date ☐☐ / ☐☐

Signature _____

name _____

address _____

_____

_____

town/city _____

post code _____

country _____

POST TO:
MUTE, Unit 9, The Whitechapel Centre
85 Myrdle St., London E1 1HL, UK

Or call our credit card hotline 020 7377 6949.
Fax 020 7377 9520

Web http://www.metamute.org/product
Email mute@metamute.org

www.ingramcontent.com/pod-product-compliance
Lightning Source LLC
Chambersburg PA
CBHW030811180526
45163CB00003B/1238